Welles-Turner
Memorial Library
Glastonbury, CT 06033

W9-BVG-867

everyday grain-free baking

Over 100 Recipes for Deliciously Easy Grain-Free and Gluten-Free Baking

Kelly Smith

DISCARDED BY
WELLES-TURNER
MEMORIAL LIBRARY
GLASTONBURY, CT

adamsmedia
Avon, Massachusetts

Copyright © 2015 by Kelly Smith.
All rights reserved.
This book, or parts thereof, may not be reproduced in any form without permission from the publisher; exceptions are made for brief excerpts used in published reviews.

Published by
Adams Media, a division of F+W Media, Inc.
57 Littlefield Street, Avon, MA 02322. U.S.A.
www.adamsmedia.com

ISBN 10: 1-4405-7436-7
ISBN 13: 978-1-4405-7436-8
eISBN 10: 1-4405-7437-5
eISBN 13: 978-1-4405-7437-5

Printed in the United States of America.

10   9   8   7   6   5   4   3   2   1

Many of the designations used by manufacturers and sellers to distinguish their products are claimed as trademarks. Where those designations appear in this book and F+W Media, Inc. was aware of a trademark claim, the designations have been printed with initial capital letters.

This book is intended as general information only, and should not be used to diagnose or treat any health condition. In light of the complex, individual, and specific nature of health problems, this book is not intended to replace professional medical advice. The ideas, procedures, and suggestions in this book are intended to supplement, not replace, the advice of a trained medical professional. Consult your physician before adopting any of the suggestions in this book, as well as about any condition that may require diagnosis or medical attention. The author and publisher disclaim any liability arising directly or indirectly from the use of this book.

Always follow safety and commonsense cooking protocol while using kitchen utensils, operating ovens and stoves, and handling uncooked food. If children are assisting in the preparation of any recipe, they should always be supervised by an adult.

Photography by Kelly Smith.
Cover design by Jessica Pooler.
Cover photo by Kelly Smith.

This book is available at quantity discounts for bulk purchases.
For information, please call 1-800-289-0963.

DEDICATION

This simple, beautiful book is dedicated to real everyday families like yours and mine. I hope it will be a bright ray of sunshine that enables each of us to more easily bring those old familiar favorites back to the table with a delightful simplicity that leaves our lives less stressed and more centered on enjoying the people God has brought into our lives.

CONTENTS

REDISCOVERING THE JOY OF BAKING

My passion for cooking and baking has its roots in a childhood filled with large family gatherings that always centered around a table overflowing with delicious Southern-style food. With conversations and laughter filling the air as familiar favorites were passed among us, I soon came to realize that sharing a meal was more than just passing the biscuits—it was about passing on memories, family traditions, and cherished moments in each other's lives.

As my husband and I started our new life together, I wanted to recreate the experiences of my childhood in making our kitchen table the hub of our home, and pass on to our children the familiar comfort foods and traditions that I knew and loved as a child. Everything was right on track with this dream when suddenly our lives changed. In 2007, I began to suffer from two chronic autoimmune disorders—interstitial cystitis and irritable bowel syndrome. Not long afterward, I was diagnosed with gluten sensitivity as well. Yet, despite several prescription medications, I was still in constant pain and discomfort.

I soon came to realize that a healthier way to find relief was to radically overhaul my diet. Like many others, I felt quite overwhelmed by the unfamiliar dietary restrictions required as I strove to regain my health. Weighing even heavier upon my heart was how to continue the tradition of family gatherings around simple and delicious meals at the kitchen table.

Thankfully, many new friends came into my life who inspired me with their knowledge about the whole-food lifestyle, as well as gluten-free, grain-free living. As I learned to translate everything I knew and loved about cooking into a more whole-food, nutrient-dense approach, amazing health transformations began to take place—both in my life and in the lives of my family members.

These positive changes did not go unnoticed, and soon I was sharing my rapidly growing knowledge, experience, and passion for healthy grain-free living with friends far and wide. With the support of my family, I launched TheNourishingHome.com—a whole-food, grain-free lifestyle blog dedicated to helping individuals and families live a more nourished life!

Although many of us live with the challenge of adhering to various dietary restrictions, by no means should these restrict us from experiencing the joy of sharing cherished traditions with our family and friends.

Therefore, my heartfelt mission in writing this book is to provide you with a whole host of deliciously comforting grain-free baking recipes, while also inspiring you to rediscover the joy of sharing your delightful creations with those you love. With the easy, delicious recipes found throughout this book, your kitchen can once again become a welcome gathering place for you, your family, and friends, to break bread and share your lives with one another.

INTRODUCTION

Living grain-free doesn't mean you have to sacrifice your favorite baked goods. In fact, each one of the more than 100 easy-to-make recipes found in Everyday Grain-Free Baking *is the result of my passion to take the everyday comfort foods we each hold dear and reinvent them so that they're not only acceptable grain-free substitutes for old favorites, but are so delightfully flavorful that you won't even notice that anything is missing.*

As a firm believer in the whole-food lifestyle, I've made sure that each scrumptious recipe—from Easy Everyday Bread and Sweet Cinnamon Roll Biscuits to Raspberry Crumble Bars and Deep Dish Apple Pie—utilizes only real food ingredients. No processed or refined foods and no starch-based flours are included. The result is a healthier, more nutrient-rich baked good that will leave you and your family feeling satisfied with every tasty bite!

In addition, I've also come to discover that there is no one-size-fits-all grain-free diet. Instead, what works for one person may not work for another, since we're all complex, unique individuals. Therefore, this cookbook isn't focused on exploring the various nuances of one particular diet or another, but instead provides simple, grain-free baking recipes that meet the foundational elements of the most common grain-free diets. Helpful information about each of the grain-free ingredients used in this book is located in the "Grain-Free Pantry Essentials" section in Chapter 1 for easy reference. So whether you're gluten-free, grain-free, or just want to reduce your carbohydrate intake, my mission in this book is to provide you with easy and delicious recipes that your whole family can enjoy whether or not everyone is living a grain-free lifestyle.

INGREDIENTS AND ICONS

As you likely know, there are several different types of grain-free diets, each with its own dietary guidelines. As you'll soon discover, this easy-to-use cookbook is compatible with the most common grain-free diets, since it's filled with delicious baking recipes that are grain-free, gluten-free, starch-free, and free of refined sugar. The vast majority are also dairy-free, or contain dairy-free recommendations so they can easily be converted as such. To help you more easily identify which recipes are suitable for your personal dietary preferences, you'll find the following icons next to each recipe:

Dairy Free: (DF)

Dairy-Free Option Provided: (DFO)

Egg Free: (EF)

Nut Free: (NF)

Suitable for the Specific Carbohydrate Diet: (SCD)

Of course, it's not necessary to be grain-free to enjoy the scrumptious recipes in this book. That's because they've been specifically developed to appeal to everyone. So I invite you to join me for a delicious culinary adventure to discover a new twist on traditional baked-good favorites. I'm certain your taste buds and your body will appreciate the delectable grain-free, gluten-free recipes found throughout *Everyday Grain-Free Baking*. Enjoy!

Tips & Tidbits

The majority of recipes in this book are suitable for the Specific Carbohydrate Diet (SCD)—a grain-free, lactose-free, starch-free, and refined sugar–free diet centered on real, unprocessed foods. Yet, whichever dietary lifestyle you opt to follow, it's important to seek out a trusted healthcare professional to help guide you throughout your journey.

Chapter 1

THE GRAIN-FREE KITCHEN

When it comes to creating delicious grain-free baked goods, having the right ingredients on hand makes all the difference. That's because the type and quality of ingredients used, as well as the techniques for combining them, impact the ultimate success of a recipe. In this chapter, you'll find an overview of the grain-free ingredients used to create the scrumptious recipes in this book, along with recommendations for helpful baking tools. In addition, you'll receive information on the many benefits of grain-free baking and lots of tips for making your grain-free baking adventures a success. All of these details have been provided to ensure that your grain-free baking experience is a smooth and enjoyable one. So please take a moment to read through this chapter to learn the important strategies for maximizing your success in the kitchen.

As you'll soon discover, grain-free baking doesn't have to be a complicated, time-consuming process. The recipes shared throughout this book are easy to prepare and require just a few key ingredients and simple techniques. Yet, despite their simplicity, these delightful treats are so flavorful and reminiscent of their traditional namesakes that most often your loved ones will never know that what you're serving is grain-free.

WHY BAKE GRAIN-FREE?

Before we start baking, let's first take a look at the many wonderful benefits that come from learning to bake grain-free, including:

✳ **Nutritional Benefits:** Since grain-free baking does not require the use of highly processed or refined starch-based ingredients, it's a wholesome option for individuals who are striving to reduce their carbohydrate intake while increasing protein and fiber in their diet.

✳ **Naturally Gluten-Free:** For those living gluten-free, grain-free baking is an excellent whole-food option, since all of the real food ingredients used to create grain-free baked goods are naturally gluten-free.

✳ **Ease and Convenience:** Grain-free baking does not require multiple flours, or the use of starch-based binders, which makes it a quick and easy method for preparing tasty gluten-free baked goods.

✳ **Delicious Results:** Grain-free baked goods have tastes and textures remarkably similar to those of traditional gluten-based foods. In fact, grain-free baked goods are so flavorful and satisfying, many people are surprised to learn that what you're serving is gluten-free and grain-free.

Tips & Tidbits

Although the name of the book is Everyday Grain-Free Baking, my intention is not to imply that these recipes should be an all-day part of one's diet. Instead, as is the case with any baked good (grain-free or not), they should be enjoyed in moderation with the bulk of one's diet centered on a wide variety of beneficial whole foods such as vegetables, fruits, grass-fed meats and eggs, cultured foods such as yogurt, healthy fats, and other nutrient-dense foods.

GRAIN-FREE PANTRY ESSENTIALS

Making delightfully healthy grain-free baked goods is a snap with just a few key ingredients. By stocking your pantry with these real-food baking essentials, you'll be ready to make every recipe in this book. For information on where to find these grain-free baking staples and more, please see the Resources section in Appendix A at the back of the book.

Blanched Almond Flour

Blanched almond flour is made from skinless almonds that are finely ground into flour. The result is a protein-rich, gluten-free, grain-free flour with a mild, slightly sweet flavor that is perfect for creating delicious, wholesome baked goods. After testing various brands, I personally use and recommend Honeyville blanched almond flour because its extremely fine grind results in much lighter, fluffier, and tastier baked goods.

Coconut Flour

Coconut flour is made from finely ground dried coconut meat, making it another terrific grain-free option. It's high in fiber and therefore requires a much higher liquid-to-flour ratio. Because coconut is technically not a nut, coconut flour is generally a good option for those with nut sensitivities. Of course, it's important to confer with your allergist. You'll notice that I use coconut flour in nearly every almond flour recipe in this book, since it helps to absorb excess moisture and further lighten the texture of grain-free baked goods.

Coconut Butter

Coconut butter, also referred to as coconut cream concentrate, is made from whole coconut flesh that is puréed into a thick, healthy spread full of rich coconut flavor. Coconut butter is the perfect ingredient for making dairy-free icings and frostings that are smooth and creamy, and that hold up well at room temperature.

Unrefined Virgin Coconut Oil

Unrefined virgin coconut oil is a highly beneficial fat extracted from coconut meat. It not only tastes great, but it's also an excellent nondairy choice for cooking and baking, which is why it's a key ingredient in the recipes throughout this book. A good source for unrefined virgin coconut oil is Tropical Traditions brand.

Coconut Milk

Pure coconut milk is a delicious nondairy alternative to whole milk that is made by puréeing together the water and meat of a coconut. It's important to note that only pure canned coconut milk (in BPA-free cans) is recommended. So for best results, do not substitute with coconut milk beverages, since they contain unhealthy additives and fillers. Also, be sure to thoroughly whisk canned coconut milk before using it in a recipe, since the cream often separates from the water.

Palm Shortening

Palm shortening is made from nonhydrogenated palm oil and is an excellent nondairy substitute for butter. Its light, nearly flavorless texture makes it an excellent option for baking, and it also works well for creating smooth, creamy frostings and icings that hold up well at room temperature.

Baking Soda

Baking soda is the leavening agent of choice for grain-free, starch-free baking. Although baking soda is an alkaline compound, when mixed with acidic ingredients (such as lemon juice or vinegar), it reacts by releasing bubbles of carbon dioxide that help baked goods to rise. It's important to note that baking powder is not the same as baking soda, so the two cannot be used interchangeably.

Grass-Fed Butter

Note that the majority of recipes in this book are dairy-free, or have dairy-free options, such as coconut oil or palm shortening. However, for those who can tolerate dairy, grass-fed butter is a tasty, highly nutritious fat. When it comes to baking, it's important to only use unsalted butter, since it provides the necessary fat without changing the flavor of a recipe.

Unflavored Gelatin

Unflavored gelatin is a healthy starch-free option for thickening and binding ingredients, such as those used in custards, puddings, and pie crusts. A good source for grass-fed gelatin is Great Lakes brand.

Honey

Local raw honey is my go-to sweetener of choice, which is why you'll find it used in the majority of the recipes in this book. When it comes to baking, I recommend using a mild honey such as sage or clover. The robust flavor of honeys such as orange blossom and wildflower varieties are often too strong and can overpower delicate baked goods.

Coconut Crystals

Coconut crystals, also known as coconut sugar, come from the sap of the coconut palm flower. They are a low-glycemic, unrefined alternative to processed sugar that has a light sweet flavor similar to brown sugar. Although honey is my preferred sweetener, I occasionally use coconut crystals, particularly in cookie recipes since they help to create a much crisper cookie.

Apple Cider Vinegar

Using apple cider vinegar is a healthy way to increase the acidity in recipes, which is especially important in baking, since an acid medium used in conjunction with baking soda helps contribute to a better rise. Apple cider vinegar is recommended over other varieties because its mild flavor doesn't leave a hint of vinegary taste behind, even in the most delicate baked goods.

Sea Salt

Cooking and baking with a high-quality fine-ground sea salt truly makes a difference in terms of taste and outcome, not to mention its superior nutritional benefits. That's because sea salt is unrefined and contains many essential trace minerals. Brands such as Real Salt or Celtic Sea Salt are good choices.

Raw Cashew Butter

Raw cashews and raw cashew butter are common ingredients used in grain-free baking because of their mild flavor and ultra-creamy texture. You'll find creamy raw cashew butter to be the key ingredient for making light and fluffy grain-free sandwich breads and rolls that taste remarkably similar to gluten-based breads.

Yogurt

Plain yogurt—made from either whole milk or coconut milk—is an excellent ingredient to have on hand to add richness, moisture, and acidity to a variety of baking recipes. The use of yogurt results in lighter, fluffier baked goods, which is why you'll find recipes for homemade Whole Milk Yogurt and Coconut Milk Yogurt in Chapter 10.

Chocolate

Enjoying dark chocolate (preferably fair-trade) on occasion is a special treat. For grain-free baking, it's best to use nonalkalized, gluten-free cocoa powders such as Dagoba. When it comes to chocolate chips, Enjoy Life mini chocolate chips are an excellent option, since they are free of gluten, dairy, and soy.

HELPFUL BAKING TOOLS

Investing in quality bakeware makes grain-free baking much easier and more successful too! These key baking essentials are my personal favorites for creating delicious grain-free baked goods, which is why they're often called for within this book. By having these helpful tools on hand, you'll have the exact equipment necessary to successfully make every recipe in this book.

Baking Basics

* Measuring Cups and Spoons
* Mixing Bowls
* Offset Spatula
* Rubber Spatulas
  (spoon-shape and thin jar spatula)
* Whisks
  (large and small balloon whisks)
* Microplane Zester
* Parchment Paper
* Parchment Muffin Cup Liners

Baking Dishes

* 8" × 8" Baking Dish
* 9" × 9" Baking Dish
* 9" Deep-Dish Pie Dish

Baking Pans

* 8.5" × 4.5" Loaf Pan
* 9" Tart Pan
* Baking Sheet/Cookie Sheet
* 12-Cup Muffin Tin

Baking Tools

* Blender
* Food Processor
* Stand Mixer
  (or electric hand mixer)

For information on the exact bakeware products I use, be sure to visit my online store at TheNourishingHome.com.

READY, SET, BAKE! STRATEGIES FOR MAXIMIZING YOUR SUCCESS

You've probably been there . . . A photo of a beautiful recipe entices you to start baking, only to discover your creation looks nothing like the photo. What went wrong? In this section, you'll find some basic strategies to help ensure that all of your grain-free creations are as beautiful and delicious as the pictures that inspired you to make them—in this book and wherever else your grain-free baking adventures lead you.

Be a Follower First, an Adventurer Second

It's important to note that the recipes in this book have been thoroughly tested multiple times to ensure a consistent outcome. So the first rule of thumb when it comes to maximizing your success is to follow the recipes exactly as written. This means curbing any impulse to make substitutions or measurement changes, or to skip steps, as each of these changes will invariably impact the outcome of a recipe, often producing a less than desirable result. Instead, first make the recipe exactly as written. Then if you're feeling adventurous, make minor adjustments the next time around based on your taste preferences.

This is particularly important when it comes to baking. That's because the type of ingredients and how they are combined must be carefully planned to ensure they work together harmoniously to create the proper moisture, rise, and texture that make baked goods light, fluffy, and delicious.

Use the Right Tools for the Job

Similarly, it's important to use the correct tools called for in a recipe. For example, if a recipe calls for an 8" × 8" baking dish, substituting with a larger pan will result in a thinner baked good that may be overdone, if the bake time is not adjusted. Also, using a whisk to do the job of a stand mixer (or electric hand mixer) will not only result in quite an upper-body workout, but may lead to ingredients not being properly combined, which will ultimately impact the outcome of a recipe.

Remember Your *Mise en Place*

Mise en place is a French culinary term that refers to the practice of having each ingredient ready to go before you start making a recipe. That way, you don't have to stop to do anything other than add the next ingredient.

To get started, first read a recipe through in its entirety. This will help you determine what steps you need to do first in order to have all of the ingredients ready to go before you start combining them. For example, you may need to dice fruit for muffins, or cut butter into small pieces for scones. Trust me, if you adopt the practice of gathering and preparing all of your ingredients in advance of starting a recipe, you will find life in the kitchen not only quicker and easier, but more successful and enjoyable too!

Fluff, Scoop, and Sweep

When it comes to measuring grain-free flours, always use the standard "fluff, scoop, and sweep" method when making the recipes in this book, since correct measuring is vital for successful baking. Simply fluff the flour using a fork and dip your measuring cup into the fluffed flour to scoop it up. Then, sweep the top of the measuring cup using the back of a knife to level the flour.

Freshness Is Key!

For best results, fresh flour is essential. Grain-free flour should ideally be purchased in sealed packages from a quality provider, since lengthy exposure to air can greatly impact freshness and moisture levels. Therefore, once you open a package of grain-free flour, consider storing a 2-week supply in an airtight container in your pantry for convenience. Then store the remaining flour in an airtight container in the fridge or freezer to maintain long-term freshness. In general, grain-free flours can be stored in the refrigerator for up to 1 month, and in the freezer for up to 6 months.

Note: If you store your flour in the refrigerator or freezer, be sure to bring it to room temperature before measuring it out in a recipe, since cold flour can negatively impact the outcome of a recipe.

When it comes to baking, getting the best—and tastiest—results requires knowing your oven and how to properly use it.

One of the first things to determine is how accurate your oven is in reaching the proper temperature, since an oven that doesn't run true to temperature is often the cause of burnt biscuits or undercooked cakes. Using a quality oven thermometer can help you determine whether your oven runs hot, cold, or true to temperature.

Similarly, preheating your oven is a crucial step in baking success. It's highly important for an oven to be at proper baking temperature before a dish goes into the oven in order for it to cook evenly. Additionally, try to resist the urge to continually open the oven door to check a dish's progress, since this allows a lot of heat to escape. Instead, if you know that your oven is true to temperature, it's best to wait until the minimum bake time is reached (as noted in the recipe) before opening the oven door to check. The exception, of course, is when a peek through the window reveals a dish that's browning sooner than expected.

And last, but not least . . . For the recipes in this book, unless otherwise specified, your oven rack should be placed in the middle position for even baking. This is especially important when it comes to grain-free ingredients like nut flours and honey, which can burn easily.

LET'S GET STARTED!

Now that you've learned a few key strategies for grain-free baking success, it's time to get started. Remember, the simplicity of the ingredients and easy-to-follow instructions for combining them not only make the recipes within this book perfect for everyday baking; they also help to ensure delicious results that are remarkably similar to the taste and texture of traditional baked goods. So put on your apron, and let's have some fun baking together!

Chapter

2

BREADS AND ROLLS

Easy Everyday Bread

Makes 1 Loaf

Living grain-free doesn't mean missing out, especially when it comes to bread. This delicious cashew butter bread will trick your taste buds into believing it's the real deal, as it has a remarkable likeness in both taste and texture to traditional bread. It's light and airy with a slightly crunchy crust.

¾ cup blanched almond flour

1 tablespoon coconut flour

1 teaspoon baking soda

½ teaspoon sea salt

1¼ cups unsalted creamy raw cashew butter

2 large eggs, plus 3 egg whites

1 teaspoon honey

2 tablespoons water

1 tablespoon apple cider vinegar

1. Preheat oven to 315°F. Grease an 8.25" x 4.25" loaf pan and line bottom only with parchment paper, slightly greasing the parchment as well. (**Note:** A standard 9" x 5" loaf pan will result in a loaf with less height. But it will still taste great!)

2. In a small bowl, combine the almond flour, coconut flour, baking soda, and salt; set aside.

3. In a large mixing bowl, add the cashew butter, eggs, egg whites, and honey. Using a stand mixer or electric hand mixer, blend together until smooth and creamy.

4. Add the water to the nut butter mixture and mix until well blended.

5. Add the dry ingredients to the wet and mix until batter is smooth and creamy, making sure to scrape down the bowl as needed.

6. Mix in the apple cider vinegar, then pour batter into the prepared loaf pan using a rubber spatula to scrape all the batter from the bowl.

7. Bake for approximately 40 minutes, until golden brown and a toothpick inserted into center comes out clean.

8. Allow bread to rest on stovetop about 10 minutes. Then run a knife along the edges and invert onto a cutting board to finish cooling.

9. Once bread has completely cooled, use a serrated bread knife to slice and serve. Bread can be wrapped and stored in an airtight container in fridge for about 5–7 days, or frozen for 2–3 months.

Tips & Tidbits

Not a fan of bread heels? Use them to make homemade bread crumbs. Simply cube the bread and dry it out for several hours in a 200°F oven. Allow to cool, then process in a blender. Store in an airtight container in your freezer until ready to use in your favorite recipes.

Cinnamon Swirl Bread

Makes 1 Loaf

With its light, fluffy texture and slightly sweet swirls of rich cinnamon goodness, this delightful bread makes a beautiful and tasty addition to any breakfast or brunch. It's perfect toasted with a pat of butter, and it's even better when used to make French toast.
(See Recipe Variation for more information.)

CINNAMON SWIRL

1½ tablespoons unsalted butter (or coconut oil), melted

2 tablespoons honey

1½ teaspoons ground cinnamon

BREAD

¾ cup blanched almond flour

1 tablespoon coconut flour

1 teaspoon baking soda

¼ teaspoon sea salt

1¼ cups unsalted creamy raw cashew butter

2 large eggs, plus 3 egg whites

1 tablespoon honey

1 tablespoon water

1 teaspoon pure vanilla extract

2 teaspoons apple cider vinegar

Optional: ⅓ cup raisins

1. Preheat oven to 315°F. Grease an 8.25" × 4.25" loaf pan and line bottom only with parchment paper, slightly greasing the parchment as well. (**Note:** A standard 9" × 5" loaf pan will result in a loaf with less height. But it will still taste great!)

2. **For the Cinnamon Swirl:** In a small bowl, whisk together the cinnamon swirl ingredients—melted butter (or coconut oil), honey, and cinnamon; set aside.

3. **For the Bread:** In a medium bowl, combine the almond flour, coconut flour, baking soda, and salt; set aside.

4. In a large mixing bowl, add the cashew butter, eggs, egg whites, and honey. Using a stand mixer or electric hand mixer, blend together until smooth and creamy.

5. Add the water and vanilla to the nut butter mixture and mix until well blended.

6. Add the dry ingredients to the wet and mix until batter is smooth and creamy, making sure to scrape down the bowl as needed.

7. Mix in the apple cider vinegar, then fold in the raisins, if using.

8. Pour half of the batter into the prepared loaf pan. Drizzle ⅔ of the cinnamon swirl mixture over the top of the batter.

9. Pour the remaining batter into the loaf pan, using a rubber spatula to scrape all the batter from the bowl. Drizzle the top of the batter with the remaining cinnamon swirl mixture.

10. Bake for approximately 40 minutes, until golden brown and a toothpick inserted into center comes out clean.

11. Allow bread to rest on stovetop about 10 minutes. Then run a knife along the edges and invert onto a cutting board to finish cooling.

12. Once bread has completely cooled, use a serrated bread knife to slice and serve. Bread can be wrapped and stored in an airtight container in fridge for about 5–7 days, or frozen for 2–3 months.

Recipe Variation

Turn this delightful cinnamon bread into the best grain-free French toast in town. Create an egg batter for dipping the bread by whisking together 1 cup of almond or coconut milk, 3 large eggs, ½ teaspoon of pure vanilla extract, and ¼ teaspoon of ground cinnamon. Thoroughly coat both sides of the bread slices in the egg batter and place on a hot buttered griddle, cooking about 1–2 minutes per side. This will make 8 slices of French toast.

Classic Brown Bread

Makes 1 Loaf

This slightly sweet, classic brown bread with its rich molasses and rye-flavored undertones is a welcome addition to any table. It's ideal for creating hearty grilled sandwiches and paninis.

¾ cup blanched almond flour

1 tablespoon coconut flour

1 tablespoon caraway seeds, plus extra for sprinkling

1 teaspoon baking soda

½ teaspoon sea salt

1¼ cups unsalted creamy raw cashew butter

2 large eggs, plus 3 egg whites

1 tablespoon organic unsulfured molasses

2 teaspoons pure honey

1 tablespoon water

1 tablespoon apple cider vinegar

1. Preheat oven to 315°F. Grease an 8.25" x 4.25" loaf pan and line bottom only with parchment paper, slightly greasing the parchment as well. (**Note:** A standard 9" x 5" loaf pan will result in a loaf with less height. But it will still taste great!)

2. In a small bowl, combine the almond flour, coconut flour, caraway seeds, baking soda, and salt; set aside.

3. In a large mixing bowl, add the cashew butter, eggs, egg whites, molasses, and honey. Using a stand mixer or electric hand mixer, blend together until smooth and creamy.

4. Add the water to the nut butter mixture and mix until well blended.

5. Add the dry ingredients to the wet and mix until batter is smooth and creamy, making sure to scrape down the bowl as needed.

6. Mix in the apple cider vinegar, then pour batter into the prepared loaf pan using a rubber spatula to scrape all the batter from the bowl. Sprinkle top with additional seeds, if desired.

7. Bake for approximately 40 minutes, until golden brown and a toothpick inserted into center comes out clean.

8. Allow bread to rest on stovetop about 10 minutes. Then run a knife along the edges and invert onto a cutting board to finish cooling.

9. Once bread has completely cooled, use a serrated bread knife to slice and serve. Bread can be wrapped and stored in an airtight container in fridge for about 5–7 days, or frozen for 2–3 months.

Tips & Tidbits

An easy way to ensure you've measured the correct amount of nut butter is to spoon it into a dry measuring cup and lightly tap the measuring cup on the surface of your countertop. This will result in the nut butter evenly spreading in the cup, so you can more easily fill and level it.

Pumpkin Spice Bread

Makes 1 Loaf

It wouldn't be fall without the beloved aroma and flavor of pumpkin and the spices that go along with it. This lightly sweetened Pumpkin Spice Bread allows the full flavor of pumpkin to shine through, delivering the perfect dose of quintessential fall flavors in every bite.

PUMPKIN SPICE BREAD

2 cups blanched almond flour

2 tablespoons coconut flour

1¼ teaspoons Pumpkin Pie Spice (see recipe in Chapter 10)

1 teaspoon baking soda

½ teaspoon sea salt

¾ cup pumpkin purée

⅓ cup honey

2 tablespoons coconut oil, melted

3 large eggs

2 tablespoons coconut milk

2 teaspoons pure vanilla extract

½ teaspoon apple cider vinegar

PRALINE TOPPING

¼ cup pecan pieces

1 tablespoon coconut crystals (for SCD use honey)

Sprinkle of ground cinnamon

Tips & Tidbits

Use a thin jar spatula (or your finger) to help get the thick wet ingredients—such as honey, puréed pumpkin, and yogurt—out of a dry measuring cup.

---

1. Preheat oven to 350°F. Grease an 8.25" × 4.25" loaf pan and line bottom only with parchment paper, slightly greasing the parchment as well. (**Note:** A standard 9" × 5" loaf pan will result in a loaf with less height. But it will still taste great!)

2. **For the Pumpkin Spice Bread:** In a small bowl, combine the almond flour, coconut flour, Pumpkin Pie Spice, baking soda, and salt; set aside.

3. In a large mixing bowl, add the pumpkin purée, honey, and coconut oil. Using a stand mixer or electric hand mixer, blend together until smooth and creamy.

4. Add the eggs, coconut milk, and vanilla to the pumpkin mixture and blend until well combined.

5. Add the dry ingredients to the wet and mix until batter is thick and smooth, making sure to scrape down the bowl as needed.

6. Mix in the apple cider vinegar, then pour batter into the prepared loaf pan using a rubber spatula to scrape all the batter from the bowl.

7. **For the Praline Topping:** Scatter pecan pieces across the top of the batter, followed by a sprinkling of coconut crystals (or drizzle of honey), and just a touch of ground cinnamon.

8. Bake for approximately 45 minutes, until golden brown and a toothpick inserted into center comes out clean.

9. Allow bread to rest on stovetop about 10 minutes. Then run a knife along the edges and invert onto a cutting board to finish cooling.

10. Once bread has completely cooled, use a serrated bread knife to slice and serve. Bread can be wrapped and stored in an airtight container in fridge for about 5–7 days, or frozen for 2–3 months.

Ultimate Banana Bread

Makes 1 Loaf

This easy, scrumptious banana bread is one of the most requested recipes in my home—and you'll soon find it to be the same in your home, too. Topped with a layer of sliced bananas, it truly is the ultimate in moist, delicious flavor!

2 cups blanched almond flour

2 tablespoons coconut flour

1 teaspoon baking soda

½ teaspoon sea salt

1 cup mashed ripe banana (about 2 large ripe bananas)

3 tablespoons honey

2 tablespoons coconut oil, melted

3 large eggs

2 tablespoons coconut milk

2 teaspoons pure vanilla extract

1 teaspoon apple cider vinegar

Optional: 1 tablespoon of coconut oil, melted

Optional: 1 large ripe banana, sliced

1. Preheat oven to 350°F. Grease an 8.25" x 4.25" loaf pan and line bottom only with parchment paper, slightly greasing the parchment as well. (**Note:** A standard 9" x 5" loaf pan will result in a loaf with less height. But it will still taste great!)

2. In a small bowl, combine the almond flour, coconut flour, baking soda, and salt; set aside.

3. In a large mixing bowl, add the mashed banana, honey, and 2 tablespoons of coconut oil. Using a stand mixer or electric hand mixer, blend together until smooth and creamy.

4. Add the eggs, coconut milk, and vanilla to the banana mixture and blend until well combined.

5. Add the dry ingredients to the wet and mix until batter is thick and smooth, making sure to scrape down the bowl as needed.

6. Mix in the apple cider vinegar, then pour batter into the prepared loaf pan using a rubber spatula to scrape all the batter from the bowl.

7. Optional: In a medium bowl, add 1 tablespoon of melted coconut oil. Cut 1 banana into thin slices and gently toss in the coconut oil until well coated. Arrange the banana slices along the top of the batter, leaving the center open for even baking.

8. Bake bread for approximately 45 minutes, until golden brown and a toothpick inserted into center comes out clean.

9. Allow bread to rest on stovetop about 10 minutes. Then run a knife along the edges and invert onto a cutting board to finish cooling.

10. Once bread has completely cooled, use a serrated bread knife to slice and serve. Bread can be wrapped and stored in an airtight container in fridge for about 5–7 days, or frozen for 2–3 months.

Recipe Variation

....

If you're a chocolate lover, fold ⅓ cup of dairy-free mini chocolate chips into the batter. This bread is also enhanced by the addition of walnuts, either sprinkled across the top of the bread, or folded into the batter—or both!

Sandwich Rounds

Makes 6 Buns

These spectacular sandwich rounds are sure to become one of your personal favorites. Tired of biscuit-tasting buns, I was inspired to adapt my Easy Everyday Bread (see recipe in this chapter) to create a real breadlike-tasting bun that can stand up to a pile of sandwich fillings, or a juicy burger hot off the grill.

⅔ cup blanched almond flour

1 tablespoon coconut flour

½ teaspoon baking soda

½ teaspoon sea salt

1 cup unsalted creamy raw cashew butter

2 large eggs, plus 2 egg whites

½ teaspoon honey

1 tablespoon water

1 tablespoon apple cider vinegar

Optional: Seeds of your choice, such as sesame, poppy, or caraway

1. Preheat oven to 315°F. Grease a 6-cup mini-pie pan. (See Tips & Tidbits for other options.)

2. In a small bowl, combine the almond flour, coconut flour, baking soda, and salt; set aside.

3. In a large mixing bowl, add the cashew butter, eggs, egg whites, and honey. Using a stand mixer or electric hand mixer, blend together until smooth and creamy.

4. Add the water to the nut butter mixture and mix until well blended.

5. Add the dry ingredients to the wet and mix until batter is smooth and creamy, making sure to scrape down the bowl as needed.

6. Mix in the apple cider vinegar, then evenly divide batter among the pie wells in the prepared mini-pie pan. (See Tips & Tidbits for other options.) If desired, sprinkle tops with your choice of seeds, such as sesame, poppy, or caraway.

7. Bake for approximately 15–18 minutes, until golden brown and a toothpick inserted into center comes out clean.

8. Allow sandwich rounds to rest on stovetop about 5 minutes. Then run a knife along the edges and invert onto a cutting board to finish cooling.

9. Once they've completely cooled, use a serrated bread knife to slice them in half and top with your favorite sandwich fillings or burger. Sandwich rounds can be wrapped and stored in an airtight container in fridge for about 5–7 days, or frozen for 2–3 months.

Tips & Tidbits

If you don't have a mini-pie tin, no worries! You can use individual ramekins, or mini quiche or tart pans. Just remember, you may need to adjust the bake time based on the size of the baking dish. For deeper dishes such as ramekins, you'll need to increase the bake time by a few minutes. For wider, shallower dishes, such as mini-tart pans, a shorter bake time may be required.

Classic Dinner Rolls

Makes 12 Rolls

These light and fluffy dinner rolls taste like real bread because they're a slightly modified version of the scrumptious Easy Everyday Bread recipe found earlier in this chapter. They're so good that even your non-grain-free family and friends will reach for seconds when you bake up a batch of these tasty rolls.

½ cup blanched almond flour
1 tablespoon coconut flour
1 teaspoon baking soda
½ teaspoon sea salt
1 cup unsalted creamy raw cashew butter
2 large eggs, plus 2 egg whites
1 teaspoon honey
1 tablespoon water
1 tablespoon apple cider vinegar

1. Preheat oven to 315°F. Grease a 12-cup muffin tin; set aside.

2. In a small bowl, combine the almond flour, coconut flour, baking soda, and salt; set aside.

3. In a large mixing bowl, add the cashew butter, eggs, egg whites, and honey. Using a stand mixer or electric hand mixer, blend together until smooth and creamy.

4. Add the water to the nut butter mixture and mix until well blended.

5. Add the dry ingredients to the wet and mix until batter is smooth and creamy, making sure to scrape down the bowl as needed.

6. Mix in the apple cider vinegar, then evenly divide batter among the muffin cups, making sure to only fill each cup halfway.

7. Bake for approximately 15–18 minutes, until golden brown and a toothpick inserted into center comes out clean.

8. Allow rolls to rest on stovetop about 5 minutes. Then run a knife along the edges and invert onto a cutting board and serve warm.

9. Rolls can be refrigerated for 5–7 days in an airtight container, or kept frozen for 2–3 months. To rewarm, thaw first, then place in a 200°F oven for 3–5 minutes.

Recipe Variation

Create flavorful variations to this classic roll by folding in 1–2 teaspoons of fresh minced garden herbs to the batter. Or top with your favorite seeds, such as sesame or poppy.

Chile-Cheese "Corn" Bread

(SCD)

Makes 10 Muffins

These slightly sweet and savory "corn bread" muffins taste so close to the real deal that you'd almost swear there's corn in them. Enjoy these with your favorite hearty chili, soups, or stews.

2 cups blanched almond flour

2 tablespoons coconut flour

¾ cup shredded extra sharp Cheddar cheese

1 teaspoon baking soda

½ teaspoon sea salt

⅛ teaspoon dry mustard

¼ cup unsalted butter, melted

2 teaspoons pure honey

3 large eggs

⅓ cup plain Whole Milk Yogurt
   (see recipe in Chapter 10)

½ teaspoon apple cider vinegar

1 tablespoon finely diced green chiles (or
   1–2 teaspoons seeded, fine-diced jalapeños)

Optional: Jalapeño slices for garnish

1. Preheat oven to 350°F. Place 10 parchment muffin liners into a 12-cup muffin tin; set aside.

2. If using, slice the jalapeño into rounds, making sure to remove the seeds from the slices; set aside.

3. In a food processor, add the almond flour, coconut flour, Cheddar cheese, baking soda, salt, and dry mustard. Process on low until well combined. Set aside.

4. In a large bowl, whisk together the melted butter and honey until creamy. Then whisk in the eggs, yogurt, and apple cider vinegar until well combined.

5. Add the dry ingredients to the wet, whisking to ensure no lumps remain.

6. Use a rubber spatula to fold in the fine-chopped green chiles (or fine-diced jalapeños).

7. Evenly distribute the batter among the muffin cups and, if you wish, top each with a jalapeño slice for the cute factor.

8. Bake for approximately 20–25 minutes, until slightly browned around edges and a toothpick inserted into center comes out clean. Allow muffins to cool in tin about 5 minutes, then serve warm with your favorite soups, stews, and chili.

Tips & Tidbits

Green chiles add a tangy depth of flavor to the muffins. However, if you prefer a little heat, toss in some fine-diced jalapeños. Just remember, when using jalapeños, less is more, unless you really like it hot.

Cheddar-Herb Coconut Flour Rolls

Makes 8 Rolls

These flavorful, herb-infused Cheddar rolls make the perfect addition to your favorite soups and stews, and also complement the rich flavor of roasted meats. Serve them warm, for a melt-in-your-mouth sensation!

¼ cup unsalted butter, softened

4 large eggs, room temperature

¼ cup, plus 1 teaspoon coconut flour

½ teaspoon baking soda

½ teaspoon garlic powder

¼ teaspoon sea salt

½ cup shredded sharp Cheddar cheese

2 teaspoons fresh minced herbs
(see Recipe Variation for suggestions)

1. Preheat oven to 375°F. Place 8 parchment muffin liners into a 12-cup muffin tin; set aside.

2. In a medium mixing bowl, whisk together the butter and eggs until smooth and creamy.

3. Sift in the coconut flour, baking soda, garlic powder, and salt, and whisk well until thoroughly combined with no lumps remaining.

4. Fold in the cheese and minced herbs. Then evenly divide batter among the 8 muffin cups.

5. Bake for approximately 12–15 minutes, until a toothpick inserted into center comes out clean.

6. Allow rolls to rest on stovetop for just 2–3 minutes. Then transfer to wire rack to finish cooling. Remove paper liners and place in bread basket. Serve warm for best flavor and texture.

Recipe Variation

These rolls are so versatile, you can add virtually any fresh herbs you have on hand, such as chives, dill, rosemary, or thyme. If substituting with dried herbs, reduce the amount to ½ to 1 teaspoon, depending on the strength of the herb.

Pizza Crust

Makes 1 10" Crust

It's funny how when you can't have something, suddenly you crave it. This recipe came about as a result of a deep hankering for a slice of pizza pie. This tasty Pizza Crust stands up well to a boatload of toppings, allowing you to enjoy one of the simplest of comfort foods without the gluten and grain that typically go along with it.

2 large eggs

2 tablespoons olive oil

2 teaspoons coconut flour

2 cups blanched almond flour

¼ teaspoon baking soda

¼ teaspoon dried Italian herb seasoning

¼ teaspoon garlic powder

¼ teaspoon sea salt

Optional: 3 tablespoons grated Parmesan cheese (omit if dairy-free)

1. Preheat oven to 350°F. Lightly oil a pizza stone, or line a large baking sheet with parchment paper; set aside.

2. In a large mixing bowl, whisk together the eggs and olive oil until well blended. Then add the coconut flour and whisk until no lumps remain.

3. Using a spoon, stir in the almond flour, baking soda, and seasonings, plus the Parmesan cheese, if using. Continue stirring until you form a dough ball.

4. Flatten the dough onto the prepared baking surface. Cover with a sheet of parchment, then evenly roll out to form a 10" circle.

5. Bake for 12–15 minutes, until lightly browned along edges.

6. Top with your favorite toppings and bake for another 8–10 minutes. Use a pizza cutter to slice; serve warm.

Chapter

3

BISCUITS, SCONES, AND CRACKERS

Southern-Style Biscuits

Makes 8 Biscuits

Growing up in the South, I have fond memories of warm biscuits gracing our table not only at breakfast time but often at dinnertime as well. My desire for this simplest of comfort foods led to the birth of this almond flour biscuit recipe that has become one of the most popular recipes on my blog. Top them with a pat of butter and a drizzle of sweet honey, or your favorite homemade preserves.

2½ cups blanched almond flour

½ teaspoon baking soda

¼ teaspoon sea salt

3 tablespoons unsalted butter (or coconut oil), melted

1 tablespoon honey

2 tablespoons coconut milk

2 large eggs

¼ teaspoon apple cider vinegar

1. Preheat oven to 350°F. Line a baking sheet with parchment paper; set aside.

2. In a small bowl, combine almond flour, baking soda, and salt.

3. In a medium bowl, whisk together melted butter (or coconut oil) and honey until smooth. Add the coconut milk, eggs, and apple cider vinegar, whisking together until well combined.

4. Using a spoon, stir the dry mixture into the wet mixture until thoroughly combined.

5. For quick and easy drop biscuits: Drop biscuit dough by large spoonfuls onto the prepared baking sheet, placing biscuits approximately 2" apart.

6. For classic round biscuits: Scoop a large spoonful of batter into your hands and roll into a ball about the size of an apricot; repeat until you have made 8. Place the dough balls on the parchment-lined baking sheet and gently flatten using the palm of your hand.

7. Bake about 15 minutes, until golden brown on top and a toothpick inserted into center comes out clean. Serve warm with butter, raw honey, or homemade jam.

Strawberry Shortcake Biscuits

Makes 6 Biscuits

Although most strawberry shortcake recipes call for some type of pound cake or angel food cake as the base, a proper shortcake is basically a big, sweet biscuit, which is what you'll find in this authentic Southern-style shortcake. Fill this beauty with some fresh, ripe strawberries and a dollop of Whipped Coconut Cream for a wholesome sweet treat that is sure to bring a smile to everyone's face.

BISCUITS

2½ cups blanched almond flour

½ teaspoon baking soda

¼ teaspoon sea salt

¼ cup unsalted butter (or coconut oil), melted

1 tablespoon pure honey

2 large eggs

¼ teaspoon pure vanilla extract

STRAWBERRY TOPPING

1 pound fresh ripe strawberries

1 tablespoon honey (or maple syrup)

Optional: **Whipped Coconut Cream** (see recipe in Chapter 10)

1. Preheat oven to 350°F. Line a baking sheet with parchment paper; set aside.

2. **For the Biscuits:** In a small bowl, combine almond flour, baking soda, and salt.

3. In a medium bowl, whisk together melted butter (or coconut oil) and honey until smooth. Add the eggs and vanilla, whisking together until well combined.

4. Using a spoon, stir the dry mixture into the wet mixture until thoroughly combined. Place dough in fridge to cool about 10 minutes.

5. **For the Strawberry Topping:** Slice the strawberries and toss with honey (or maple syrup). If using, prepare the Whipped Coconut Cream.

6. Once biscuit dough is chilled, scoop a large spoonful of batter into your hands and roll into a ball about the size of an apricot; repeat until you have made 6. Place the dough balls on the parchment-lined baking sheet and gently flatten using the palm of your hand.

7. Bake about 15 minutes, until golden brown on top and a toothpick inserted into center comes out clean.

8. Split warm biscuits in half and top with a couple of heaping spoonfuls of strawberry topping and a dollop of Whipped Coconut Cream, if desired. A delightful treat for breakfast or dessert!

Recipe Variation

In the summer when peaches are in season, try topping these scrumptious biscuits with fresh ripe peach slices and some homemade Whipped Coconut Cream. Heavenly!

Coconut Flour Drop Biscuits

Makes 10 Biscuits

*Almost cakelike in taste and texture, these easy-to-make drop biscuits are a tasty treat.
Their delicate flavor pairs beautifully with a drizzle of honey or
a dab of homemade preserves.*

⅓ cup coconut flour
½ teaspoon baking soda
¼ teaspoon sea salt
¼ cup unsalted butter (or coconut oil), softened
1 tablespoon honey
4 large eggs
¼ teaspoon apple cider vinegar

1. In a small bowl, combine the coconut flour, baking soda, and salt.

2. In a medium bowl, whisk together softened butter (or coconut oil) and honey until smooth. Then add the eggs and apple cider vinegar, whisking together until well combined.

3. Sift the dry mixture into the wet mixture, and whisk well until thoroughly combined with no lumps remaining. Refrigerate dough for 30 minutes, until completely chilled.

4. Meanwhile, preheat oven to 375°F about 15 minutes before dough is ready to come out of fridge. Line a baking sheet with parchment paper.

5. Once dough is chilled, drop biscuit dough by large spoonfuls onto the prepared baking sheet, placing biscuits approximately 2" apart. (See Tips & Tidbits for more information.)

6. Bake about 10–12 minutes, until a toothpick inserted into center comes out clean. Top with a drizzle of raw honey or a dab of homemade preserves.

Tips & Tidbits

To keep these Coconut Flour Drop Biscuits from spreading too thin, it's important to thoroughly chill the dough. Also, do not flatten the dough when you scoop it. Instead, leave it nice and tall, since these will spread during baking.

Garden Herb Biscuits

Makes 6 Biscuits

These light and fluffy, yet filling, biscuits are a delightful way to make use of your favorite fresh herbs. These savory little fellows are the perfect accompaniment to hearty wintertime soups and stews, as well as simple roasted meats.

2½ cups blanched almond flour

½ cup shredded sharp Cheddar cheese (or 1 tablespoon palm shortening, if dairy-free)

1½ teaspoons finely minced fresh herbs of your choice

½ teaspoon baking soda

¼ teaspoon sea salt

⅛ teaspoon garlic powder

2 large eggs

¼ cup coconut milk

¼ teaspoon apple cider vinegar

1. Preheat oven to 350°F. Line a baking sheet with parchment paper; set aside.

2. In a food processor, combine almond flour, Cheddar cheese (or palm shortening), herbs, baking soda, salt, and garlic powder. Pulse a few times until the cheese is well blended into the flour. If you don't have a food processor, use a pastry cutter to incorporate the cheese (or palm shortening) into the flour.

3. In a large bowl, whisk together the eggs, coconut milk, and apple cider vinegar until well combined. Using a spoon, stir the dry mixture into the wet mixture until thoroughly combined.

4. Scoop a large spoonful of batter into your hands and roll into a ball about the size of an apricot; repeat until you have made 6. Place the dough balls on the parchment-lined baking sheet and gently flatten using the palm of your hand.

5. Bake about 15 minutes, until golden brown on top and a toothpick inserted into center comes out clean. Serve warm with butter. These make the perfect accompaniment to hearty soups and stews.

Tips & Tidbits

You can add just about any fresh herbs you have on hand to this biscuit dough. I like to use a combination of thyme, rosemary, and parsley. If substituting with dried herbs, reduce the amount to ½ to 1 teaspoon, depending on the strength of the herb.

Sweet Cinnamon Roll Biscuits

Makes 6–8 Biscuits

One of the beautiful aspects of food is how the simple aroma or taste of a particular ingredient can conjure fond memories of days of old. Nearly any time I catch the scent of cinnamon and walnuts baking together, I flash back to Sunday mornings as a child enjoying cinnamon rolls with my family. These Sweet Cinnamon Roll Biscuits help the memory live on, and are well worth the extra time it takes to prepare this recipe, since it's handmade with love.

BISCUITS

2½ cups blanched almond flour

½ teaspoon baking soda

¼ teaspoon sea salt

¼ teaspoon ground cinnamon

¼ cup unsalted butter, softened, (or palm shortening)

1 tablespoon pure honey

½ teaspoon pure vanilla extract

2 large eggs

2 teaspoons coconut flour

½ teaspoon apple cider vinegar

CINNAMON-WALNUT FILLING

½ cup walnut pieces

3 tablespoons honey

1 tablespoon unsalted butter (or coconut oil), melted

½ teaspoon vanilla extract

1 tablespoon ground cinnamon

Optional: Sweet Vanilla Glaze for topping (see recipe in Chapter 10)

1. **For the Biscuits:** In a small bowl, combine almond flour, baking soda, salt, and cinnamon.

2. In a large bowl, whisk together the softened butter (or palm shortening), honey, and vanilla until smooth and creamy. Then whisk in the eggs, coconut flour, and apple cider vinegar until smooth with no lumps remaining.

3. Using a spoon, stir the dry mixture into the wet mixture until thoroughly combined. Place dough in fridge to cool for 30 minutes.

4. **For the Cinnamon Walnut Filling:** Use a food processor to pulse the walnuts just until they are in small bits; set aside. In a small bowl, whisk together the honey, butter (or coconut oil), vanilla, and cinnamon; set aside.

5. Once dough is chilled, place it on a sheet of parchment paper and use your hands to form a flat square. Place another sheet of parchment on top of the dough and roll it out to about a 10" × 12" rectangle about ¼" thick.

6. Drizzle top of dough with honey-cinnamon mixture. Then sprinkle top with walnut bits.

7. Carefully roll the dough into a log starting from one of the short ends. I've found the easiest way to do this is to gently lift one side of the parchment paper and have gravity help you. As you lift the paper with one hand, use your other hand's fingers to slowly roll the dough into a tight log. Then transfer the log to the fridge to chill at least 1 hour, or overnight.

8. Once dough log is completely chilled, preheat oven to 325°F. Line a baking sheet with parchment paper; set aside.

9. Carefully use a sharp knife to cut the log into 1" rounds. Transfer the cinnamon roll biscuits to the prepared baking sheet and allow them to come to room temperature.

10. Bake about 18–22 minutes, until golden brown around the edges. Allow the biscuits to cool on baking sheet until they're just slightly warm. Then drizzle with Sweet Vanilla Glaze, if using, and enjoy.

Tips & Tidbits

Starting a simple tradition of serving a favorite food on a designated day, such as birthdays or special holidays, not only gives your family something delicious to look forward to, but also builds fond memories that last a lifetime!

Blueberry Lemon Scones

Makes 8 Scones

While in London for a visit, I enjoyed my first afternoon tea. I'll never forget that charming tearoom with its bounty of lovely finger sandwiches, scones, and teacakes. Perhaps you've longed for a delectable scone with your cup of tea, too? Good news: This delightful recipe captures the taste and texture of a classic Southern-style scone, which makes it the perfect companion at teatime.

2¾ cups blanched almond flour, plus 1 handful for flouring workspace

½ teaspoon baking soda

¼ teaspoon sea salt

2 tablespoons cold unsalted butter (or palm shortening)

2 large eggs

2 tablespoons coconut milk

2 teaspoons lemon juice

1 teaspoon lemon zest

2 teaspoons honey

⅓ cup dried blueberries

1 teaspoon butter or coconut oil

Optional: Coconut crystals or maple sugar for sprinkling on top (omit for SCD)

1. In a food processor, combine the almond flour, baking soda, and salt. Pulse in the cold butter (or palm shortening) until it's well incorporated. If you don't have a food processor, use a pastry cutter (or 2 knives) to cut the butter (or shortening) into the flour.

2. In a large bowl, whisk together the eggs, coconut milk, lemon juice, zest, and honey until well combined.

3. Using a spoon, stir the dry mixture into the wet mixture until thoroughly combined. Then fold in the blueberries. Place dough in fridge to cool about 10–15 minutes.

4. Preheat oven to 350°F while dough is chilling. Line a baking sheet with parchment paper; set aside. Sprinkle your work surface with a handful of blanched almond flour. Melt 1 teaspoon of butter or coconut oil for brushing the tops of the scones.

5. Once dough is chilled, gather it together in a ball and place it on the floured surface. Shape the dough into a square about 6" × 6" and 1" thick, then cut it in half twice to form 4 small squares. Next, cut each of the 4 small squares in half diagonally to form 8 small triangles.

6. Brush the tops of the scones with a little melted butter or coconut oil. Sprinkle tops with a little bit of coconut crystals or maple sugar, if desired.

7. Using a spatula, gently place each scone onto the prepared baking sheet. Bake about 15–18 minutes, until scones are light golden brown along the edges.

8. Serve warm with your favorite herbal or green tea.

Tips & Tidbits

The dried blueberries used in this recipe really enhance the slight natural sweetness of these scones. But you can certainly substitute fresh blueberries, if you prefer.

Cranberry Orange Scones

(DFO) (SCD)

Makes 8 Scones

The bold flavor combination of tart cranberries paired with sweet orange zest is a traditional favorite, especially during the holiday season. This simply delightful scone captures these festive flavors, making it the perfect accompaniment to your favorite holiday gatherings.

2¾ cups blanched almond flour, plus 1 handful for flouring workspace

½ teaspoon baking soda

¼ teaspoon sea salt

2 tablespoons cold unsalted butter (or palm shortening)

2 large eggs

2 tablespoons coconut milk

2 teaspoons orange juice

1 teaspoon orange zest

2 teaspoons honey

⅓ cup dried cranberries

1 teaspoon butter or coconut oil

Optional: Coconut crystals or maple sugar for sprinkling on top (omit for SCD)

1. In a food processor, combine the almond flour, baking soda, and salt. Pulse in the butter or palm shortening until it's well incorporated. If you don't have a food processor, use a pastry cutter (or 2 knives) to cut the butter (or shortening) into the flour.

2. In a large bowl, whisk together the eggs, coconut milk, orange juice, zest, and honey until well combined.

3. Using a spoon, stir the dry mixture into the wet mixture until thoroughly combined. Then fold in the cranberries. Place dough in fridge to cool about 10–15 minutes.

4. Preheat oven to 350°F while dough is chilling. Line a baking sheet with parchment paper; set aside. Sprinkle your work surface with a handful of blanched almond flour. Melt 1 teaspoon of butter or coconut oil for brushing the tops of the scones.

5. Once dough is chilled, gather it together in a ball and place it on the floured surface. Shape the dough into a square about 6" x 6" and 1" thick, then cut it in half twice to form 4 small squares. Next, cut each of the 4 small squares in half diagonally to form 8 small triangles.

6. Brush the tops of the scones with a little melted butter or coconut oil. Sprinkle tops with a little bit of coconut crystals or maple sugar, if desired.

7. Using a spatula, gently place each scone onto the prepared baking sheet. Bake about 15–18 minutes, until scones are light golden brown along the edges.

8. Serve warm with your favorite herbal or green tea.

Cherry Chocolate Chip Scones

(DFO)

Makes 8 Scones

Dried cherries and chocolate chips are a wonderful flavor combination. The juxtaposition of tartness and sweetness makes these scones a true delight for teatime or anytime.

2¾ cups blanched almond flour, plus 1 handful for flouring workspace

½ teaspoon baking soda

¼ teaspoon sea salt

2 tablespoons cold unsalted butter (or palm shortening)

2 large eggs

3 tablespoons coconut milk

2 teaspoons honey

¼ cup dried cherries

2–3 tablespoons dairy-free mini chocolate chips

1 teaspoon butter or coconut oil

Optional: Coconut crystals or maple sugar for sprinkling on top

1. In a food processor, combine the almond flour, baking soda, and salt. Pulse in the butter (or palm shortening) until it's well incorporated. If you don't have a food processor, use a pastry cutter (or 2 knives) to cut the butter (or shortening) into the flour.

2. In a large bowl, whisk together the eggs, coconut milk, and honey until well combined.

3. Using a spoon, stir the dry mixture into the wet mixture until thoroughly combined. Then fold in the cherries and chocolate chips. Place dough in fridge to cool about 10–15 minutes.

4. Preheat oven to 350°F while dough is chilling. Line a baking sheet with parchment paper; set aside. Sprinkle your work surface with a handful of blanched almond flour. Melt 1 teaspoon of butter or coconut oil for brushing the tops of the scones.

5. Once dough is chilled, gather it together in a ball and place it on the floured surface. Shape the dough into a square about 6" × 6" and 1" thick, then cut it in half twice to form 4 small squares. Next, cut each of the 4 small squares in half diagonally to form 8 small triangles.

6. Brush the tops of the scones with a little melted butter or coconut oil. Sprinkle tops with a little bit of coconut crystals or maple sugar, if desired.

7. Using a spatula, gently place each scone onto the prepared baking sheet. Bake about 15–18 minutes, until scones are light golden brown along the edges.

8. Serve warm with your favorite herbal or green tea.

Simple Garden Herb Crackers

(DF) (SCD)

Makes 50–60 Crackers

This basic cracker recipe was developed with versatility in mind! Not only is this recipe great with fresh or dried herbs, but it can also be used to create other delicious flavor combinations, such as the popular Multi-Seed Crackers and Rosemary Raisin Crackers, also featured in this chapter. These savory little crackers are great solo, or when served with your favorite healthy dips and toppings.

2 cups blanched almond flour

1 teaspoon dried minced onion

½ teaspoon of your favorite dried herbs (see Recipe Variation for suggestions)

½ teaspoon sea salt, plus more to sprinkle on crackers, if desired

1 tablespoon olive oil

1 large egg

1 teaspoon filtered water

1. Preheat oven to 350°F. In a small bowl, combine almond flour, dried onion, herbs, and sea salt.

2. In a large bowl, whisk together olive oil, egg, and water until well blended.

3. Using a spoon, stir dry ingredients into wet mixture until thoroughly combined. Use your hands to knead the dough into a ball.

4. Place the dough ball between 2 large sheets of parchment paper and roll out to about ⅛" thickness.

5. Remove top piece of parchment paper. Using a pizza cutter or sharp knife, trim the dough to form an even rectangle shape. Set aside scraps.

6. Cut dough into 2" × 2" squares. Do not remove cut dough squares. Instead, transfer the entire sheet of parchment with cut dough onto the baking sheet.

7. Make a small dough ball out of the scraps and re-roll and cut. Place on a second baking sheet and, if desired, lightly sprinkle crackers with a touch of sea salt.

8. Bake for approximately 12 minutes, until crackers along the outer edge of the baking sheet are light golden brown. Then turn off oven and open the oven door just a crack. Leave it open to allow majority of heat to escape while the crackers finish crisping up (about 1–2 minutes).

9. Remove crackers from oven and allow them to cool. Often the crackers in the center of the baking sheet will still be a bit chewy. If so, remove the crispy crackers and place the rest back into the oven while it's still warm. Do not turn the oven on; simply close the door and peek in on them every few minutes to ensure they do not overbrown.

10. To keep crackers crispy, store in an airtight container in the freezer. You can eat them cold straight from the freezer, or bring to room temperature before serving.

Recipe Variation

....

These crackers are wonderfully versatile, since you can add virtually any dried herbs you have on hand, such as thyme, Herbes de Provence, Italian seasoning mix, rosemary, etc. If using fresh herbs, be sure to mince them first and increase the measurement to 1 teaspoon.

Rosemary Raisin Crackers

Makes 50–60 Crackers

If you're a fan of sweet and savory, then this is the cracker for you! Not only are these beauties an absolute treat on their own, but they're especially delightful when paired with your favorite tangy, grass-fed cheese.

2 cups blanched almond flour

2 tablespoons finely diced raisins

½ teaspoon dried rosemary

½ teaspoon sea salt, plus more to sprinkle on crackers, if desired

1 tablespoon olive oil

1 large egg

1 teaspoon filtered water

1. Preheat oven to 350°F. In a small bowl, combine almond flour, diced raisins, dried rosemary, and sea salt.

2. In a large bowl, whisk together olive oil, egg, and water until well blended.

3. Using a spoon, stir dry ingredients into wet mixture until thoroughly combined. Use your hands to knead the dough into a ball.

4. Place the dough ball between 2 large sheets of parchment paper and roll out to about ⅛" thickness.

5. Remove top piece of parchment paper. Using a pizza cutter or sharp knife, trim the dough to form an even rectangle shape. Set aside scraps.

6. Cut dough into 2" × 2" squares. Do not remove cut dough squares. Instead, transfer the entire sheet of parchment with cut dough onto the baking sheet.

7. Make a small dough ball out of the scraps and re-roll and cut. Place on a second baking sheet and, if desired, lightly sprinkle crackers with a touch of sea salt.

8. Bake for approximately 12 minutes, until crackers along the outer edge of the baking sheet are light golden brown. Then turn off oven and open the oven door just a crack. Leave it open to allow majority of heat to escape while the crackers finish crisping up (about 1–2 minutes).

9. Remove crackers from oven and allow them to cool. Often the crackers in the center of the baking sheet will still be a bit chewy. If so, remove the crispy crackers and place the rest back into the oven while it's still warm. Do not turn the oven on; simply close the door and peek in on them every few minutes to ensure they do not overbrown.

10. To keep crackers crispy, store in an airtight container in the freezer. You can eat them cold straight from the freezer, or bring to room temperature before serving.

Multi-Seed Crackers

Makes 50–60 Crackers

Made with your choice of savory seeds, these little crackers are so flavorful, you'll be tempted to eat the entire batch! Good thing almond flour crackers are a healthier option to traditional starch-based, gluten-free brands since they contain a good dose of protein, fiber, and nutrients in each tasty bite.

2 cups blanched almond flour

5 teaspoons of your favorite seeds
   (see Tips & Tidbits for suggestions)

1 teaspoon dried minced onion

½ teaspoon sea salt, plus more to sprinkle on crackers, if desired

1 tablespoon olive oil

1 large egg

1 teaspoon filtered water

Tips & Tidbits

You can use any type of seeds you like, such as chia, poppy, sesame, caraway, etc. If using sunflower seeds, give them a rough-chop first to decrease their size. One of our favorite combos is 3 teaspoons sesame seeds, 2 teaspoons poppy seeds, and 1 teaspoon caraway seeds.

1. Preheat oven to 350°F. In a small bowl, combine almond flour, seeds, dried onion, and sea salt.

2. In a large bowl, whisk together olive oil, egg, and water until well blended.

3. Using a spoon, stir dry ingredients into wet mixture until thoroughly combined. Use your hands to knead the dough into a ball.

4. Place the dough ball between 2 large sheets of parchment paper and roll out to about ⅛" thickness.

5. Remove top piece of parchment paper. Using a pizza cutter or sharp knife, trim the dough to form an even rectangle shape. Set aside scraps.

6. Cut dough into 2" × 2" squares. Do not remove cut dough squares. Instead, transfer the entire sheet of parchment with cut dough onto the baking sheet.

7. Make a small dough ball out of the scraps and re-roll and cut. Place on a second baking sheet and, if desired, lightly sprinkle crackers with a touch of sea salt.

8. Bake for approximately 12 minutes, until crackers along the outer edge of the baking sheet are light golden brown. Then turn off oven and open the oven door just a crack. Leave it open to allow majority of heat to escape while the crackers finish crisping up (about 1–2 minutes).

9. Remove crackers from oven and allow them to cool. Often the crackers in the center of the baking sheet will still be a bit chewy. If so, remove the crispy crackers and place the rest back into the oven while it's still warm. Do not turn the oven on; simply close the door and peek in on them every few minutes to ensure they do not overbrown.

10. To keep crackers crispy, store in an airtight container in the freezer. You can eat them cold straight from the freezer, or bring to room temperature before serving.

Cheddar Cheese Crackers

(SCD)

Makes 50–60 Crackers

Those bright orange square crackers can't compare with this real-food version that combines wholesome blanched almond flour with tangy Cheddar cheese. The result is an amazingly tasty cracker that may have you eating the entire batch in just one sitting. Consider yourself warned.

2 cups blanched almond flour

½ teaspoon sea salt, plus more to sprinkle on crackers, if desired

¼ teaspoon dry mustard

¼ teaspoon paprika

1 cup shredded sharp Cheddar cheese

2 egg whites

2 teaspoons olive oil

1. Preheat oven to 350°F.

2. In a food processor, combine the almond flour, sea salt, dry mustard, and paprika. Pulse in the cheese until it's well blended into the flour. If you don't have a food processor, use a pastry cutter to incorporate the cheese into the flour.

3. Pulse in the egg whites and oil until a dough ball forms. (Or whisk the egg whites and oil together and stir them into the dry ingredients using a spoon.)

4. Use your hands to knead the dough into a ball. Place the dough ball between 2 large sheets of parchment paper and roll out to about ⅛" thickness.

5. Remove top piece of parchment paper. Using a pizza cutter or sharp knife, trim the dough to form an even rectangle shape. Set aside scraps.

6. Cut dough into 2" × 2" squares. Do not remove cut dough squares. Instead, transfer the entire sheet of parchment with cut dough onto the baking sheet.

7. Make a small dough ball out of the scraps and re-roll and cut. Place on a second baking sheet and, if desired, lightly sprinkle crackers with a touch of sea salt.

8. Bake for approximately 12 minutes, until crackers along the outer edge of the baking sheet are light golden brown. Then turn off oven and open the oven door just a crack. Leave it open to allow majority of heat to escape while the crackers finish crisping up (about 1–2 minutes).

9. Remove crackers from oven and allow them to cool. Often the crackers in the center of the baking sheet will still be a bit chewy. If so, remove the crispy crackers and place the rest back into the oven while it's still warm. Do not turn the oven on; simply close the door and peek in on them every few minutes to ensure they do not overbrown.

10. To keep crackers crispy, store in an airtight container in the freezer. You can eat them cold straight from the freezer, or bring to room temperature before serving.

Chapter

4

MUFFINS

Apple Streusel Muffins

Makes 8 Muffins

This gem of a recipe celebrates the delightful marriage of apples with cinnamon, resulting in a muffin that will have you singing "Mmmm!" with every scrumptious bite!

MUFFINS

2¼ cups blanched almond flour

2 teaspoons coconut flour

½ teaspoon baking soda

¼ teaspoon sea salt

2 large eggs

⅓ cup plain Whole Milk Yogurt or Coconut Milk Yogurt (see recipes in Chapter 10)

1 tablespoon honey

1 tablespoon lemon juice

1½ teaspoons pure vanilla extract

CINNAMON STREUSEL TOPPING

2 tablespoons honey

1 tablespoon unsalted butter (or coconut oil), melted

2½ teaspoons ground cinnamon

¼ teaspoon pure vanilla extract

½ cup diced organic apple (about 1 small apple)

½ cup walnut pieces

1. Preheat oven to 315°F. Place 8 parchment muffin liners into a 12-cup muffin tin; set aside.

2. **For the Muffins:** In a small bowl, combine the almond flour, coconut flour, baking soda, and salt. In a large bowl, whisk together the eggs, yogurt, honey, lemon juice, and vanilla until well blended. Using a spoon, stir the dry ingredients into the wet and mix until well blended. Set batter aside.

3. **For the Cinnamon Streusel Topping:** In the small bowl used for the dry ingredients (so you'll have fewer dishes to do), add the streusel ingredients except for the diced apple and walnuts. Whisk together until well combined. Set aside.

4. Add a large spoonful of muffin batter to each of the lined muffin cups, making sure to fill no more than ⅓ of the muffin liner. Gently tap the muffin tin on the counter, or use moistened fingers to evenly distribute the batter in the bottom of the muffin cups.

5. Using a small spoon, place a dollop of the streusel in the center of each muffin and top with a little sprinkling of diced apple and walnuts.

6. Place another large spoonful of batter on top of the cinnamon-apple-nut layer, making sure to evenly distribute the remaining batter among all the muffin cups.

7. Top each muffin with the remaining diced apple and nuts. Then drizzle the remaining cinnamon streusel over the top of each muffin.

8. Bake for approximately 22–25 minutes, until a toothpick inserted into center comes out clean. Allow muffins to cool in the tin for 5–10 minutes. Serve warm.

Chocolate-Covered Banana Muffins

(DF)

Makes 10 Muffins

Similar to cupcakes, these muffins are perfect for a special occasion. Their decadent dark chocolate flavor is enhanced by the sweet sensation of ripe banana. And of course, the addition of a chunk of banana planted firmly in the center, drizzled with a little honey, just adds to their irresistible charm.

2 cups blanched almond flour

½ teaspoon baking soda

¼ teaspoon sea salt

¾ cup mashed ripe banana (about 2 medium bananas)

3 tablespoons honey, plus more for drizzling over muffins before baking

¼ cup cocoa powder (preferably fair-trade cocoa)

2 large eggs

1 tablespoon coconut milk

2 teaspoons pure vanilla extract

½ teaspoon apple cider vinegar

¼ cup dairy-free mini chocolate chips

1 large semi-ripe banana, cut into 10 thick slices

1. Preheat oven to 350°F. Place 10 parchment muffin liners into a 12-cup muffin tin; set aside.

2. In a small bowl, combine the almond flour, baking soda, and salt.

3. In a large bowl, whisk together the mashed banana and honey until well blended. Then add the cocoa powder, eggs, coconut milk, vanilla, and apple cider vinegar. Whisk until cocoa powder is thoroughly blended into the mixture.

4. Using a spoon, stir the dry ingredients into the wet and mix until well blended. Then fold in the chocolate chips and evenly distribute the batter among the 10 muffin cups.

5. Insert a banana slice into the center of each muffin, so that only half of the slice is visible. Drizzle a little honey over the top of the banana (about ½ teaspoon per muffin), if desired.

6. Bake for approximately 20–25 minutes, until a toothpick inserted into center comes out clean. Allow muffins to cool in the tin for 5–10 minutes. Then transfer to a plate and serve.

Strawberry Shortcake Muffins

Makes 8 Muffins

These delightful muffins were inspired by my neighbors' children, who love to come over and bake with me and my boys. This recipe is super easy to make and provides a wonderful opportunity to teach children basic baking skills. In fact, these muffins are so delicious, we shared the recipe on my blog as part of the Kids in the Kitchen series, which encourages families to cook together.

2¼ cups blanched almond flour

2 teaspoons coconut flour

½ teaspoon baking soda

¼ teaspoon sea salt

2 large eggs

⅓ cup plain Whole Milk Yogurt or Coconut Milk Yogurt (see recipes in Chapter 10)

2 tablespoons honey

2 teaspoons lemon zest (about 1 lemon)

1 tablespoon lemon juice

½ teaspoon pure vanilla extract

½ cup finely diced fresh strawberries

1. Preheat oven to 315°F. Place 8 parchment muffin liners into a 12-cup muffin tin; set aside.

2. In a small bowl, combine the almond flour, coconut flour, baking soda, and salt.

3. In a large bowl, whisk together the eggs, yogurt, honey, lemon zest, lemon juice, and vanilla until well blended.

4. Using a spoon, stir the dry ingredients into the wet and mix until well blended. Then fold in the diced strawberries and evenly distribute the batter among the 8 muffin cups.

5. Bake for approximately 22–25 minutes, until a toothpick inserted into center comes out clean. Allow muffins to cool in the tin for 5–10 minutes. Then transfer to a wire rack to finish cooling.

Cranberry Pecan Streusel Muffins

(DFO)

Makes 10 Muffins

These scrumptious little upside-down cakes in a muffin tin are perfect for sharing at a brunch, party, or other special occasion. They're so easy to make and always get rave reviews!

CRANBERRY PECAN STREUSEL

3 tablespoons unsalted butter (or coconut oil), melted

3 tablespoons coconut crystals

1¼ teaspoons ground cinnamon

⅓ cup pecan pieces

¾ cup quartered fresh cranberries (or thawed frozen cranberries)

MUFFINS

2 cups blanched almond flour

1 teaspoon coconut flour

½ teaspoon baking soda

¼ teaspoon sea salt

2 large eggs

3 tablespoons plain Whole Milk Yogurt or Coconut Milk Yogurt (see recipes in Chapter 10)

1 tablespoon honey

1 tablespoon lemon juice

1 teaspoon pure vanilla extract

1. Preheat oven to 350°F. Place 10 parchment muffin liners into a 12-cup muffin tin; set aside.

2. **For the Cranberry Pecan Streusel:** In a medium bowl, whisk together the melted butter (or coconut oil), coconut crystals, and cinnamon until well combined. Stir in the pecans and quartered cranberries. Evenly divide the streusel along the bottom of the 10 muffin cups. Set muffin tin aside.

3. **For the Muffins:** In a small bowl, combine the almond flour, coconut flour, baking soda, and salt. In a large bowl, whisk together the eggs, yogurt, honey, lemon juice, and vanilla until well blended. Using a spoon, stir the dry ingredients into the wet and mix until well blended.

4. Spoon the muffin batter over the top of the streusel, making sure to evenly divide it among each of the muffin cups.

5. Bake for approximately 15–20 minutes, until a toothpick inserted into center comes out clean. Allow muffins to cool in the tin for 5–10 minutes. Then transfer to a wire rack to finish cooling.

6. Gently remove the paper liners from each muffin and place them on a serving tray with the cranberry-pecan streusel side facing up.

Favorite Fruit Muffins

Makes 8 Muffins

These simple muffins are so versatile! Nearly any fruit you have on hand tastes great in these slightly sweet almond muffins, which is why I refer to them as "odds 'n' ends" muffins. That's because they're perfect for repurposing leftover fruit from fruit salads, the fruit bowl, and the crisper to make individual muffins with "a little of this and little of that."

2¼ cups blanched almond flour

2 teaspoons coconut flour

½ teaspoon baking soda

¼ teaspoon sea salt

2 large eggs

⅓ cup plain Whole Milk Yogurt or Coconut Milk Yogurt (see recipes in Chapter 10)

2 tablespoons honey

1 tablespoon lemon juice

1 teaspoon pure vanilla extract

¾ cup finely diced fresh fruit (see Recipe Variation for more information)

1. Preheat oven to 315°F. Place 8 parchment muffin liners into a 12-cup muffin tin; set aside.

2. In a small bowl, combine the almond flour, coconut flour, baking soda, and salt.

3. In a large bowl, whisk together the eggs, yogurt, honey, lemon juice, and vanilla until well blended.

4. Using a spoon, stir the dry ingredients into the wet and mix until well blended. Then fold in the diced fruit and evenly distribute the batter among the 8 muffin cups.

5. Bake for approximately 22–25 minutes, until a toothpick inserted into center comes out clean. Allow muffins to cool in the tin for 5–10 minutes. Then transfer to a wire rack to finish cooling.

Recipe Variation

These muffins taste great with just about any seasonal fruit you have on hand, such as blueberries, raspberries, or strawberries. Or let your creativity flow and toss in a combination of fruits, such as kiwi-banana or apple-cherry, for a yummy change of pace.

Cranberry Orange Muffins

Makes 8 Muffins

The sweet-tart flavor combination of cranberry and orange is a classic favorite, especially during the holidays when cranberries are in season. But you can certainly enjoy these all year long by using frozen cranberries in place of fresh. Just be sure to thaw them first for even baking.

2¼ cups blanched almond flour

2 teaspoons coconut flour

½ teaspoon baking soda

¼ teaspoon sea salt

2 large eggs

⅓ cup plain Whole Milk Yogurt or Coconut Milk Yogurt (see recipes in Chapter 10)

2 tablespoons honey

2 teaspoons orange zest (about 1 medium orange)

1 tablespoon fresh-squeezed orange juice

½ teaspoon pure vanilla extract

½ cup fresh whole cranberries (or thawed frozen cranberries)

1. Preheat oven to 315°F. Place 8 parchment muffin liners into a 12-cup muffin tin; set aside.

2. In a small bowl, combine the almond flour, coconut flour, baking soda, and salt.

3. In a large bowl, whisk together the eggs, yogurt, honey, orange zest, orange juice, and vanilla until well blended.

4. Using a spoon, stir the dry ingredients into the wet and mix until well blended. Then fold in the cranberries and evenly distribute the batter among the 8 muffin cups.

5. Bake for approximately 22–25 minutes, until a toothpick inserted into center comes out clean. Allow muffins to cool in the tin for 5–10 minutes. Then transfer to a wire rack to finish cooling.

Pumpkin Pie Muffins

Makes 8 Muffins

Beautiful leaves changing colors, big bright pumpkins growing on the vine, and the aroma of autumn spices filling your home are a few of the things you may love about the fall. These tasty little muffins capture some of the splendor of autumn and are the first treats I bake when the cool crisp breeze of fall fills the air.

1¾ cups blanched almond flour

1 teaspoon coconut flour

1¼ teaspoons Pumpkin Pie Spice (see recipe in Chapter 10)

½ teaspoon baking soda

¼ teaspoon sea salt

¾ cup pumpkin purée

⅓ cup honey (or maple syrup)

2 large eggs

¼ cup plain Whole Milk Yogurt or Coconut Milk Yogurt (see recipes in Chapter 10)

2 teaspoons pure vanilla extract

1 teaspoon apple cider vinegar

Optional: ¼ cup currants (or raisins)

Optional: ¼ cup walnut pieces

1. Preheat oven to 350°F. Place 8 parchment muffin liners into a 12-cup muffin tin; set aside.

2. In a small bowl, combine the almond flour, coconut flour, Pumpkin Pie Spice, baking soda, and salt.

3. In a large bowl, whisk together the pumpkin purée and honey (or maple syrup) until well blended. Then add the eggs, yogurt, vanilla, and apple cider vinegar. Whisk until well blended.

4. Using a spoon, stir the dry ingredients into the wet and mix until well blended. Then fold in the currants (or raisins) and walnuts, if desired, and evenly distribute the batter among the 8 lined muffin cups.

5. Bake for approximately 25–28 minutes, until a toothpick inserted into center comes out clean. Allow muffins to cool in the tin for 5–10 minutes. Then transfer to a wire rack to finish cooling.

Morning Glory Muffins

Makes 8 Muffins

A blast from the past, Morning Glory Muffins were all the rage in the '70s. This healthier whole-food version is made using nutritious coconut flour loaded with fresh pineapple, apple, and carrot. These muffins are definitely a glorious way to start your day!

½ cup organic coconut flour

½ teaspoon baking soda

¼ teaspoon sea salt

4 large eggs

¼ cup plain Whole Milk Yogurt or Coconut Milk Yogurt (see recipes in Chapter 10)

3 tablespoons honey

2 tablespoons coconut oil, melted

1 teaspoon pure vanilla extract

½ cup diced fresh pineapple

⅓ cup grated carrot

¼ cup grated apple

2 tablespoons unsweetened shredded coconut

1. Preheat oven to 350°F. Place 8 parchment muffin liners into a 12-cup muffin tin; set aside.

2. In a small bowl, mix together the coconut flour, baking soda, and salt.

3. In a large bowl, whisk together the eggs, yogurt, honey, coconut oil, and vanilla until well combined.

4. Sift the dry ingredients into the wet, and whisk well to thoroughly combine, until no lumps remain and batter begins to thicken.

5. Gently fold into the batter the diced pineapple, grated carrot, diced apple, and 1 tablespoon of the shredded coconut, and evenly distribute the batter among the 8 lined muffin cups. Then sprinkle tops with the remaining tablespoon of shredded coconut.

6. Bake for approximately 20–25 minutes, until tops and edges begin to turn a light golden brown and a toothpick inserted into center comes out clean.

7. Allow to cool in the pan for 5–10 minutes. Then serve and enjoy!

Tropical Delight Muffins

Makes 8 Muffins

These moist, tender muffins are tropically inspired and taste similar to pineapple upside-down cake. However, the only sweetener used in this recipe is a touch of honey, which allows the coconut and pineapple to take center stage.

½ cup organic coconut flour

½ teaspoon baking soda

¼ teaspoon sea salt

4 large eggs

⅓ cup plain Whole Milk Yogurt or Coconut Milk Yogurt (see recipes in Chapter 10)

2 tablespoons honey

2 tablespoons coconut oil, melted

1 teaspoon pure vanilla extract

¼ teaspoon apple cider vinegar

¾ cup diced fresh pineapple

Unsweetened shredded coconut for sprinkling on top

1. Preheat oven to 350°F. Place 8 parchment muffin liners into a 12-cup muffin tin; set aside.

2. In a small bowl, mix together the coconut flour, baking soda, and salt.

3. In a large bowl, whisk together the eggs, yogurt, honey, coconut oil, vanilla, and apple cider vinegar until well combined.

4. Sift the dry ingredients into the wet, and whisk well to thoroughly combine, until no lumps remain and batter begins to thicken.

5. Gently fold the diced pineapple into the batter and evenly divide the batter among the 8 lined muffin cups. Then sprinkle the tops with a little unsweetened shredded coconut.

6. Bake for approximately 20–22 minutes, until tops and edges begin to turn a light golden brown and a toothpick inserted into center comes out clean.

7. Allow to cool in the pan for 5–10 minutes. Then transfer to a wire rack to finish cooling.

Lemonberry Muffins

Makes 8 Muffins

Moist and delicious, these nutritious coconut flour muffins provide a burst of lemon-berry goodness in every bite! Feel free to change out the raspberries and the citrus zest used in this recipe with whatever you find in season to create your own unique flavor combinations.

½ cup coconut flour

½ teaspoon baking soda

¼ teaspoon sea salt

4 large eggs

⅓ cup plain Whole Milk Yogurt or Coconut Milk Yogurt (see recipes in Chapter 10)

3 tablespoons honey

2 tablespoons coconut oil, melted

2 teaspoons lemon zest (1 lemon)

1 tablespoon lemon juice

½ teaspoon pure vanilla extract

1 cup fresh raspberries, halved

1. Preheat oven to 350°F. Place 8 parchment muffin liners into a 12-cup muffin tin; set aside.

2. In a small bowl, mix together the coconut flour, baking soda, and salt.

3. In a large bowl, whisk together the eggs, yogurt, honey, coconut oil, lemon zest, lemon juice, and vanilla until well combined.

4. Sift the dry ingredients into the wet, and whisk well to thoroughly combine, until no lumps remain and batter begins to thicken.

5. Add a large spoonful of muffin batter to each of the lined muffin cups, making sure to fill no more than ⅓ of the muffin liner.

6. Add a few raspberry halves to the top of each muffin. Then place another large spoonful of batter on top of the raspberries, making sure to evenly distribute the remaining batter among all the muffin cups. Top each muffin with the remaining raspberries.

7. Bake for approximately 20–22 minutes, until tops and edges begin to turn a light golden brown and a toothpick inserted into center comes out clean.

8. Allow to cool in the pan for 5–10 minutes. Then transfer to a wire rack to finish cooling.

Recipe Variation

You can use easy muffin recipes like this one to create "have it your way" muffins. Fill the 8 muffin cups ⅓ of the way, as described above. Then allow your family to add their favorite fruit to the muffins. Next, evenly divide the remaining batter over the top and repeat with their personal favorite toppings. This ensures that everyone is happy when the timer sounds.

Banana Bread Muffins

Makes 10 Muffins

Think of these grain-free Banana Bread Muffins as conveniently packaged little slices of scrumptious banana bread. Using extra-ripe bananas makes these muffins so aromatic that you can almost taste them while they're baking!

2 cups blanched almond flour

2 teaspoons coconut flour

½ teaspoon baking soda

¼ teaspoon sea salt

1 cup mashed ripe banana (about 2 large ripe bananas)

3 tablespoons honey

2 large eggs

1 tablespoon coconut milk

2 teaspoons pure vanilla extract

½ teaspoon apple cider vinegar

1. Preheat oven to 350°F. Place 10 parchment muffin liners into a 12-cup muffin tin; set aside.

2. In a small bowl, combine the almond flour, coconut flour, baking soda, and salt.

3. In a large bowl, whisk together the mashed banana and honey until well blended. Then add the eggs, coconut milk, vanilla, and apple cider vinegar. Whisk until well blended.

4. Using a spoon, stir the dry ingredients into the wet and mix until well blended. Then evenly distribute the batter among the 10 lined muffin cups.

5. Bake for approximately 20–25 minutes, until a toothpick inserted into center comes out clean. Allow muffins to cool in the tin for 5–10 minutes. Then transfer to a wire rack to finish cooling.

Tips & Tidbits

Next time you have overripe bananas, mash them and place in the freezer in 1-cup measurements. That way, if you're in the mood for these Banana Bread Muffins, all you'll need to do is thaw the mashed banana and you're ready to bake!

Chapter

5

PANCAKES AND WAFFLES

Fluffy Little Almond Flour
   Pancakes (DFO) (SCD)

Banana Pancake Buddies (DF) (NF) (SCD)

Apple Cinnamon Puff
   Pancake (DFO) (NF) (SCD)

Coconut Flour Pancakes (DFO) (NF) (SCD)

Pumpkin Pancakes (DFO) (SCD)

Grab 'n' Go Pancake Muffins (DFO) (SCD)

Easy Blender Waffles (DF) (SCD)

Fluffy Little Almond Flour Pancakes

(DFO) (SCD)

Makes 18 Silver-Dollar Pancakes

Finding a light and fluffy grain-free pancake recipe can be quite a challenge, which is why these Fluffy Little Almond Flour Pancakes are the top viewed and most commented-on recipe on my blog. And after just one bite, you'll discover why this recipe is so popular!

¼ cup coconut milk

1 tablespoon honey (or maple syrup)

1 tablespoon unsalted butter (or coconut oil), melted, plus additional butter or oil for greasing the griddle

1 teaspoon pure vanilla extract

¼ teaspoon apple cider vinegar

1½ cups blanched almond flour

½ teaspoon baking soda

¼ teaspoon sea salt

3 large eggs

Optional: **Pure maple syrup, or Simple Honey-Butter Syrup (see recipe in Chapter 10)**

1. Preheat griddle over medium heat.

2. Place all of the liquid ingredients except the eggs into a blender or food processor. Then place all of the dry ingredients on top. Cover and blend on low 10–15 seconds just until combined. (Batter will be very thick.)

3. Add the eggs and blend on low about 15–20 seconds, then increase to high and blend 20–30 seconds, just until eggs are incorporated into the batter. (Do not overmix or pancakes will not be tender.)

4. Transfer the pancake batter to a bowl to make it easier to spoon out the batter.

5. Grease preheated griddle with butter (or coconut oil). Ladle 2–3 spoonfuls of batter onto the griddle to form a silver-dollar-size pancake (about 3" in diameter).

6. Cook pancakes for 1–2 minutes, until pancakes begin to dry out at edges and the bottoms are a golden brown. It's important to keep a careful eye on these pancakes, as almond flour pancakes burn easily.

7. Carefully flip and cook another 1–2 minutes until done, but not overbrowned. Serve hot off the griddle with a pat of butter and a medley of fresh berries. Top with pure maple syrup or Simple Honey-Butter Syrup.

Tips & Tidbits

Save some for later! Make a double batch and allow extra pancakes to cool. Then transfer to baking sheets and place in your freezer. Once the pancakes are frozen solid, place them in a freezer-safe container. When ready to use, there's no need to thaw, simply reheat the frozen pancakes in toaster oven at 200°F for a quick, healthy breakfast.

Banana Pancake Buddies

(DF) (NF) (SCD)

Makes 12 Pancakes

Whether it's puppy ears, bunny ears, or those famous mouse ears, there's something magical about pancakes that look like favorite little friends. When I was a kid, my mom would make pancake buddies for my brother and me, complete with chocolate chip eyes. This delicious grain-free version allows you to make pancakes in any shape you'd like, and allows your family members to create funny faces, if desired. It's wonderful how something as simple as Sunday morning pancakes can build fond memories that last a lifetime!

1 tablespoon unsalted butter (or coconut oil), melted, plus additional butter or oil for greasing the griddle

½ cup mashed ripe banana (about 1 large ripe banana)

1½ teaspoons vanilla extract

½ cup coconut milk

¼ teaspoon apple cider vinegar

⅓ cup, plus 1 tablespoon coconut flour

½ teaspoon baking soda

¼ teaspoon sea salt

Pinch of ground cinnamon

4 large eggs

Optional: Pure maple syrup, or Simple Honey-Butter Syrup (see recipe in Chapter 10)

1. Place all of the liquid ingredients except the eggs into a blender or food processor. Then place all of the dry ingredients on top. Cover and blend on low 10–15 seconds just until well combined. (Batter will be thick.)

2. Add the eggs and blend on low about 15–20 seconds, then increase to high and blend 20–30 seconds, just until eggs are incorporated into the batter. (Do not overmix or pancakes will not be tender.)

3. Transfer the pancake batter to a bowl to make it easier to spoon out the batter. Allow the batter to sit 5–10 minutes, while you preheat a skillet or griddle over medium heat.

4. When ready to cook, grease preheated skillet or griddle with butter (or coconut oil). If making pancake buddies, ladle 2–3 spoonfuls of batter onto the griddle to form a round head (about 3 " in diameter). Then use 1–2 spoonfuls of batter for each ear, depending on the size and shape of the ears. If making regular pancakes, simply ladle 2–3 spoonfuls of batter onto the griddle to form a silver-dollar-size pancake (about 3" in diameter).

5. Cook pancakes for about 2 minutes, until pancakes begin to dry out at edges and the bottoms are golden brown. Then use a large spatula to carefully lift and flip the pancakes, and cook another 1–2 minutes until done, but not overbrowned.

6. If desired, decorate your pancake buddies using the Tips & Tidbits sidebar on the following page. Then top with pure maple syrup or Simple Honey-Butter Syrup, if desired.

Tips & Tidbits

Keep the pancakes small to make it easier to flip them. To create cute faces, provide sliced bananas and chocolate chips for the eyes. Raspberries or blueberries make great noses, and a strawberry makes the perfect mouth. Set out all of the toppings and have fun making silly faces. In this case, it's okay to play with your food!

Apple Cinnamon Puff Pancake

Makes 4–5 Servings

This beautiful puffy pancake may look fancy, but it's actually easier to make than a batch of pancakes. That's because there's no need to stand over a hot griddle, since this beauty bakes in the oven, leaving you plenty of time to fry up some bacon or sausage to go with it.

PANCAKE

2 tablespoons unsalted butter (or coconut oil), melted

1 tablespoon honey

2 teaspoons vanilla extract

¾ cup coconut milk

⅓ cup, plus 1 tablespoon coconut flour

½ teaspoon baking soda

¼ teaspoon sea salt

4 large eggs

APPLE FILLING

2 tablespoons unsalted butter (or coconut oil), melted, divided

2 tablespoons honey

1 teaspoon ground cinnamon

Pinch of nutmeg

3 medium apples, peeled, cored, and sliced, divided

Optional: Pure maple syrup, or Simple Honey-Butter Syrup (see recipe in Chapter 10)

1. **For the Pancake:** Place all of the liquid ingredients except the eggs into a blender or food processor. Then place all of the dry ingredients on top. Cover and blend on low to start 10–15 seconds just until well combined. (Batter will be thick.)

2. Add the eggs and blend on low about 15–20 seconds, then increase to high and blend 20–30 seconds, just until eggs are incorporated into the batter. (Do not overmix or pancake will not be tender.) Set batter aside to thicken and preheat oven to 350°F.

3. **For the Apple Filling:** In a small bowl, mix together 1 tablespoon of melted butter (or coconut oil) with the honey, cinnamon, and nutmeg.

4. Heat a 10" or 12" oven-safe skillet over medium heat on stovetop. Add the remaining 1 tablespoon of butter (or coconut oil) to the skillet and brush the oil evenly across the bottom and up the sides of the pan.

5. Add the apple slices from 2 apples to the skillet and sauté just until softened a bit. Use a fork to arrange the apple slices evenly along the bottom of the skillet.

6. Drizzle the cinnamon filling over the apples and allow the honey to begin to gently simmer. Then turn off the heat.

7. Give the pancake batter a quick stir. Slowly pour the batter evenly over the top of the sautéed apples. Garnish top with the remaining apple slices.

8. Carefully transfer the skillet to the oven. Bake about 15 minutes at 350°F, then reduce the temperature to 300°F and bake about 5–10 minutes more. Remove from oven and allow to cool 2–3 minutes, then cut and serve. It's scrumptious as is, or with a drizzle of pure maple syrup or Simple Honey-Butter Syrup, if desired.

Coconut Flour Pancakes

Makes 16 Silver-Dollar Pancakes

The fluffier the pancake, the better. And after making way too many batches, I've found that the secret to fluffy coconut flour pancakes is making sure to do two things: Separate your eggs, so you can fold well-whipped, fluffy egg whites into the batter, and keep the pancakes small—silver-dollar size, to be exact. So if you enjoy fluffy pancakes too, you'll find these to be especially delightful.

½ cup coconut flour

1 teaspoon baking soda

¼ teaspoon sea salt

Pinch of ground cinnamon

4 large eggs

2 tablespoons unsalted butter (or coconut oil), melted, plus additional butter or oil for greasing the griddle

1 tablespoon pure honey (or maple syrup)

1 teaspoon vanilla extract

1 cup coconut milk

¼ teaspoon apple cider vinegar

Optional: Pure maple syrup, or Simple Honey-Butter Syrup (see recipe in Chapter 10); blueberries or other fruit (see Tips & Tidbits for more information)

1. Preheat griddle over medium heat.

2. In a small bowl combine the coconut flour, baking soda, salt, and pinch of cinnamon.

3. Separate the egg whites from the yolks. Place the egg whites in a medium bowl; set aside.

4. Place the egg yolks in a large bowl and whisk in the melted butter (or coconut oil). Be sure the melted butter or oil has cooled to touch before adding, to avoid creating cooked egg-yolk bits.

5. Add the honey (or maple syrup), vanilla, coconut milk, and apple cider vinegar to the egg yolk mixture and whisk well to combine.

6. Sift the dry mixture into the egg yolk mixture, whisking well to thoroughly combine, making sure there are no lumps in the batter.

7. Using a clean large wire whisk, whisk the egg whites rapidly until very foamy (about 2 minutes).

8. Use the whisk to fold the whipped egg whites into the batter, by gently turning the thick batter over and over again until well combined.

9. Grease preheated griddle with butter (or coconut oil), then ladle 2–3 spoonfuls of batter onto the griddle to form a silver-dollar-size pancake (about 3" in diameter). If desired, top each pancake with a few fresh blueberries or fruit of choice (see Tips & Tidbits for more information).

10. Cook pancakes for 1–2 minutes, until the tops begin to dry out and the bottoms are a golden brown. Then carefully flip and cook another 1–2 minutes until done, but not overbrowned. Serve hot off the griddle with butter and pure maple syrup or Simple Honey-Butter Syrup.

Tips & Tidbits

Instead of folding fruit into the pancake batter, wait until you ladle the batter onto the hot griddle. Then add a small amount of diced fruit to the top of each pancake prior to flipping.

Pumpkin Pancakes

Makes 12 Silver-Dollar Pancakes

We're quite the pumpkin aficionados in our home, so developing an almond flour pumpkin pancake was on the top of my to-do list for Fall! Thankfully, this recipe is a snap to put together and tastes just like traditionally made pumpkin pancakes, which is why each autumn-inspired bite will leave you smiling!

⅓ cup pumpkin purée

2 tablespoons unsalted butter (or coconut oil), melted, plus additional butter or oil for greasing the griddle

1 tablespoon honey (or maple syrup)

1 teaspoon pure vanilla extract

¼ teaspoon apple cider vinegar

1¼ cups blanched almond flour

1 teaspoon Pumpkin Pie Spice (see recipe in Chapter 10)

½ teaspoon baking soda

¼ teaspoon sea salt

3 large eggs

Optional: Pure maple syrup, or Simple Honey-Butter Syrup (see recipe in Chapter 10)

1. Preheat griddle over medium heat.

2. Place all of the liquid ingredients except the eggs into a blender or food processor. Then place all of the dry ingredients on top. Cover and blend on low 10–15 seconds just until well combined. (Batter will be thick.)

3. Add the eggs and blend on low about 15–20 seconds, then increase to high and blend 20–30 seconds, just until eggs are incorporated into the batter. (Do not overmix or pancakes will not be tender.)

4. Transfer the pancake batter to a bowl to make it easier to spoon out the batter.

5. Grease preheated griddle with butter (or coconut oil). Then ladle 2–3 spoonfuls of batter onto the griddle to form a silver-dollar-size pancake (about 3" in diameter).

6. Cook pancakes for 1–2 minutes, until pancakes begin to dry out at edges and the bottoms are a golden brown. It's important to keep a careful eye on these pancakes, as almond flour pancakes burn easily.

7. Carefully flip and cook another 1–2 minutes until done, but not overbrowned. Serve hot off the griddle with a pat of butter. Top with pure maple syrup or Simple Honey-Butter Syrup.

Grab 'n' Go Pancake Muffins

Makes 8 Muffins

In today's world, as much as we may strive to sit at the table for a meal, there are times when a busy schedule makes it difficult. Thankfully, there's always time for a quick, healthy breakfast with these delicious and fun Grab 'n' Go Pancake Muffins.

⅓ cup plain Whole Milk Yogurt or Coconut Milk Yogurt (see recipes in Chapter 10)

2 tablespoons unsalted butter (or coconut oil), melted

1 tablespoon honey (or maple syrup)

1 teaspoon pure vanilla extract

¼ teaspoon apple cider vinegar

1¾ cups blanched almond flour

½ teaspoon baking soda

¼ teaspoon sea salt

3 large eggs

¼ cup diced strawberries

¼ cup whole blueberries

1. Preheat oven to 350°F. Grease 8 muffin cups in a 12-cup muffin tin with coconut oil. Set aside.

2. Place all of the liquid ingredients except the eggs into a blender or food processor. Then place all of the dry ingredients on top. Cover and blend on low 10–15 seconds just until well combined. (Batter will be thick.)

3. Add the eggs and blend on low about 15–20 seconds, then increase to high and blend 20–30 seconds, just until eggs are incorporated into the batter. (Do not overmix or muffins will not be tender.)

4. Transfer the muffin batter to a bowl and fold in the berries. Evenly divide the pancake muffin batter among the 8 greased muffin cups.

5. Bake for 15–18 minutes, until slightly golden brown on top and a toothpick inserted into center comes out clean. Remove from oven and allow muffins to cool 2–3 minutes in the tin. Then run a knife around the edges of each cup and invert the pan over a sheet of parchment to remove.

Tips & Tidbits

....

These pancake muffins store well in the fridge for 3–4 days. To reheat, simply place in a 200°F oven for 3–5 minutes, until warm.

Easy Blender Waffles

Makes 4–5 Waffles

Homemade waffles are a weekend breakfast favorite! This easy recipe helps to speed up the process by using a blender to combine ingredients and more easily pour the batter into your waffle maker. For a special treat, top with a dollop of Whipped Coconut Cream (see recipe in Chapter 10) and sprinkle of cinnamon.

⅓ cup coconut milk

2 tablespoons coconut oil, melted, plus additional oil for greasing the waffle iron

1 tablespoon honey (or maple syrup)

2 teaspoons pure vanilla extract

¼ teaspoon apple cider vinegar

1¼ cups blanched almond flour

½ teaspoon baking soda

¼ teaspoon sea salt

¼ teaspoon ground cinnamon

Pinch of nutmeg

3 large eggs

Optional: Pure maple syrup, or Simple Honey-Butter Syrup (see recipe in Chapter 10)

1. Preheat waffle iron.

2. Place all of the liquid ingredients except the eggs into a blender or food processor. Then place all of the dry ingredients on top. Cover and blend on low 10–15 seconds just until well combined. (Batter will be thick.)

3. Add the eggs and blend on low about 15–20 seconds, then increase to high and blend 20–30 seconds, just until eggs are incorporated into the batter. (Do not overmix or waffles will not be tender.)

4. In a small bowl, melt some additional coconut oil for greasing the waffle iron.

5. Generously brush oil on waffle iron grids and pour waffle batter evenly into waffle iron.

6. Cook about 3–4 minutes, until waffles are light golden brown. Use a fork to help gently remove the waffles from the waffle iron, then serve with a medley of fresh berries and a drizzle of pure maple syrup or Simple Honey-Butter Syrup.

Tips & Tidbits

Since waffle irons come in all shapes and sizes, and some run hotter than others, try cooking a test waffle. By cooking just one waffle to start, you'll be able to better determine the perfect cook time based on your particular waffle iron without potentially under- or overcooking a whole batch.

Chapter

6

PIES, TARTS, AND CRISPS

Pumpkin Custard Cups

Makes 5–6 Servings

As much as we adore pumpkin pie around here, sometimes it's nice to have a lighter option—especially after a filling Thanksgiving feast! This easy-to-make, dairy-free custard rises up beautifully like a soufflé and is just as light and fluffy in texture. It boasts all the fabulous flavors of creamy pumpkin pie without the heaviness of a crust.

1½ cups pure coconut milk

⅓ cup honey

3 large eggs

¾ cup pumpkin purée

1 teaspoon Pumpkin Pie Spice (see recipe in Chapter 10)

¼ teaspoon ground cinnamon, plus extra for sprinkling on top

¼ teaspoon ground ginger

¼ teaspoon salt

1 teaspoon pure vanilla extract

2 teaspoons coconut flour

Whipped Coconut Cream (see recipe in Chapter 10)

1. Preheat oven to 350°F. Oil 5–6 ramekins with palm shortening or coconut oil.

2. In a large bowl, whisk together coconut milk and honey until well combined.

3. Whisk in the eggs, pumpkin, Pumpkin Pie Spice, seasonings, and vanilla. Add the coconut flour and continue to whisk until well combined.

4. Evenly distribute the custard into the prepared ramekins, making sure to leave at least ½" of space from the top of each cup.

5. Place the ramekins on a baking sheet and carefully transfer to the oven. Bake for 30–40 minutes, until the custard rises up and sets in middle (a slight jiggle in the center is fine, as the custard will continue to set a bit as it cools).

6. Carefully remove the custard cups from the oven and transfer to a wire rack to cool. Serve warm with a dollop of Whipped Coconut Cream and a sprinkle of cinnamon, if desired.

Double Chocolate Cream Pie

(DF)

Makes 8 Servings

Everyone loves a good story, and food can be a great catalyst for sparking wonderful memories from the past. This creamy, dairy-free treat was inspired by my Granny's famous chocolate cream pie, which was my dad's favorite. Each time it's served, my family reminisces about these two special people we miss dearly. With its rich chocolate flavor and light flaky crust, this delightful pie is certain to become a cherished tradition in your home as well!

1 Chocolate Graham Crust (see recipe in this chapter)

2¾ cups pure coconut milk

2¼ teaspoons unflavored gelatin

4 large egg yolks

⅓ cup honey

2 teaspoons pure vanilla extract

⅔ cup dairy-free mini chocolate chips

2 tablespoons cocoa powder

⅛ teaspoon sea salt

Whipped Coconut Cream for topping (see recipe in Chapter 10)

Optional: Shaved chocolate for topping

1. Make the Chocolate Graham Crust recipe, but instead of placing the crust into a tart pan for baking, place it into a lightly oiled 9" deep-dish pie pan. Then bake according to recipe instructions. Set aside to cool.

2. In a medium saucepan, add the coconut milk and sprinkle the gelatin on top of the milk. Allow the gelatin to bloom (soften) about 5–10 minutes.

3. Meanwhile, in a small bowl, whisk together the egg yolks, honey, and vanilla. Set aside.

4. Once gelatin has softened, place saucepan over medium heat. Whisk constantly until the milk and gelatin are well combined and the milk is warmed.

5. Very slowly add ½ cup of the warm milk to the yolks, whisking constantly to combine. Slowly pour the yolk mixture into the saucepan and whisk thoroughly.

6. Add the chocolate chips, cocoa powder, and salt and whisk well to combine. Bring the mixture to a gentle simmer and whisk for 2–3 minutes until mixture thickens. Then pour the custard through a fine mesh strainer into a shallow dish to cool.

7. Once cooled, pour the chocolate filling into the cooled pie crust and use an offset spatula to even out the top. Place in the refrigerator to set at least 6–8 hours.

8. When ready to serve, top with fresh Whipped Coconut Cream and chocolate shavings, if desired. Serve immediately, or refrigerate for up to 12 hours.

Tips & Tidbits

If you don't have a deep-dish pie pan, simply pour excess chocolate cream filling into a bowl and refrigerate for a luscious pudding treat.

Peek-a-Boo Pie

DF **SCD**

Makes 9 Servings

*This darling classic slab pie features fresh summer berries nestled in a bed of flaky pie crust.
By using small cookie cutters, you can allow just a small peek of the delectable
warm fruity filling that's just waiting to be devoured.*

2 Basic Pie Crusts (see recipe in this chapter)

½ cup honey

½ teaspoon pure vanilla extract

16 ounces fresh cherries, pitted and halved (about 2½ cups)

1½ cups fresh blackberries

1 tablespoon lemon juice

2 cups quartered fresh strawberries

½ teaspoon unflavored gelatin

1. Make 2 Basic Pie Crusts. Use one to form the bottom crust in a 9" x 9" baking dish. Bake at 325°F for 10–12 minutes until the crust sets and is only slightly golden brown along the edges. Leave the second pie dough disk in the fridge to use for the top of the pie later. Once the bottom crust is finished baking, leave it on the stovetop to cool while you make the pie filling.

2. In a large saucepan, add the honey and vanilla. Whisk together over medium-low heat until the mixture comes to a slight simmer.

3. Add the cherries and blackberries, gently tossing them with a large wooden spoon. Cook the fruit, stirring frequently, until the cherries are slightly softened. Then turn off the heat and stir in the lemon juice and strawberries.

4. Use a slotted spoon to transfer the cooked fruit into the prepared pie crust.

5. Measure out ⅓ cup of the fruit syrup (cooking liquid) and sprinkle with the gelatin. Allow to soften about 5 minutes while you roll out the second crust. Then whisk well to combine.

6. Preheat the oven to 325°F. Place the second pie crust between 2 sheets of parchment paper and roll out slightly larger than a 9" x 9" square. Trim to 9" x 9" and transfer the pie crust to the freezer to firm up while the oven is preheating. (Chilling the pie crust will make it easier to lift and place over the fruit filling.)

7. Pour the gelatin–fruit syrup mixture evenly over the top of the fruit and then carefully place the chilled pie crust over the fruit filling as well. Use your fingers to pinch and seal the top crust gently with the bottom crust. Then use a knife or small cookie cutters to cut out cute shapes in the top crust to allow the colorful fruit to peek out.

8. Bake the pie for approximately 20–25 minutes, until golden brown along the edges and slightly bubbly. Then remove from oven and allow pie to rest for 15–20 minutes before slicing. This will ensure that the filling has time to set.

Deep Dish Apple Pie

Makes 8 Servings

I've had a love affair with this Southern staple since I savored my first bite. But how to make it grain-free? The secret is to pre-cook the apple filling so as not to burn the delicate almond flour crust. It's so good you probably won't have leftovers. Yet, if you do, you can serve a slice for breakfast with a side of bacon and scrambled eggs. Before you laugh, consider giving it a try.

2 Basic Pie Crusts (see recipe in this chapter)

2 tablespoons water

¾ teaspoon unflavored gelatin

5 large apples (such as Honeycrisp, Pink Lady, Granny Smith, or a combo)

2 tablespoons fresh lemon juice

½ cup honey

1 teaspoon pure vanilla extract

1½ teaspoons ground cinnamon

¼ teaspoon ground nutmeg

¼ teaspoon sea salt

1. Make 2 Basic Pie Crusts. Use one to form the bottom crust in a 9" deep-dish pie dish and bake at 325°F for 10–12 minutes until the crust sets and is only slightly golden brown along the edges. Leave the second pie dough disk in the fridge to use for the top of the pie later. Once the bottom crust is finished baking, leave it on the stovetop to cool while you make the pie filling.

2. In a small prep bowl, add the water and sprinkle with the gelatin. Set aside to allow the gelatin to soften.

3. Peel, core, and thinly slice the apples. Place them in a large bowl and toss them with the lemon juice. Set aside.

4. In a large saucepan, add the honey, vanilla, spices, and salt. Whisk together over medium-low heat until the mixture comes to a slight simmer.

5. Add the apple slices, tossing them with a large wooden spoon. Cook the apples, tossing them frequently, until they are slightly softened. Then use a slotted spoon to transfer the cooked apples into a large bowl to cool.

6. Whisk the gelatin into the cooking liquid and continue to simmer until it begins to thicken into a thin syrup. Then turn off the heat and move the saucepan to a cooler area on the stovetop to cool.

7. Preheat oven to 325°F. Once the cooked apples are cool to the touch, layer them evenly across the bottom pie crust to create a neatly stacked pattern. Measure out ⅓ cup of the syrup and evenly drizzle it across the top of the apples.

8. Remove the second pie dough disk from the fridge and roll it out between 2 sheets of parchment to ¼" thickness. Use a small cookie cutter to cut shapes in the dough. Then arrange them in a pleasing pattern across the top of the pie.

9. Place the pie in the oven and bake for 15–20 minutes until the top is golden brown and the apple filling is slightly bubbly. Remove from oven and allow pie to rest for 15–20 minutes before slicing. This will ensure that your pie holds together beautifully. Then enjoy the pleasure of an amazingly delicious old-fashioned apple pie!

Peach Pie in a Jar

(DFO) (EF) (SCD)

Makes 4 Servings

I discovered the mini-pies-in-a-jar craze while browsing through Pinterest and just couldn't help but fall in love with this wonderful idea for creating beautiful individual servings of pie! This simplified version features a summer favorite—peaches—topped with a slightly crunchy Snickerdoodle cookie crust.

8 soft ripe peaches

1 batch of Snickerdoodles cookie dough, chilled (see recipe in Chapter 8)

⅛ teaspoon unflavored gelatin

1 tablespoon honey

⅛ teaspoon ground cinnamon

¼ teaspoon pure vanilla extract

1. Peel and slice peaches over a large bowl in order to catch all of the juices.

2. Fill 4 1-cup wide-mouth mason jars (or recycled 1-cup jars of your choice) with the peach slices, making sure to leave at least 1" of space at the top.

3. Pour peach juice into a measuring cup. Keep ¼ cup. If you're short, add water to make ¼ cup. Sprinkle with the gelatin and leave it to sit 5 minutes to allow the gelatin to bloom (soften).

4. Meanwhile, preheat oven to 350°F. Roll out half of the Snickerdoodle dough between 2 sheets of parchment to ¾" thickness. Use the jar lid to cut out 4 cookies; set aside. Gather dough scraps and place them back in the fridge with the remaining cookie dough.

5. Add the honey, cinnamon, and vanilla to the peach-gelatin mixture and whisk well to combine. Evenly spoon the juice over the top of the peaches in each jar.

6. Carefully top each jar with a cookie dough cut-out. Place the jars in a 9" × 9" baking dish and transfer to the oven.

7. Bake for approximately 15 minutes until the cookies are golden brown and the peach filling begins to get bubbly. Carefully remove the baking dish from the oven and allow the jars to cool until they are safe to touch. Then enjoy!

Tips & Tidbits

What to do with the extra cookie dough? Follow the instructions in the recipe to bake cookies and freeze for later. Or freeze the extra dough to use for future cookie baking.

Banana Cream Tart

Makes 8 Servings

This classic diner favorite gets a fabulous dairy-free, grain-free makeover that will leave you wanting more. Each swoon-worthy bite features a delightful medley of flaky pie crust topped with sweet ripe banana slices smothered in a velvety vanilla cream filling with a thick layer of Whipped Coconut Cream. Get ready to hear: "One more slice, please!"

1 Honey Graham Crust, chilled (see recipe in this chapter)

3 large bananas, divided

1 (13.5-ounce) can of pure coconut milk (1¾ cups)

1 teaspoon coconut butter

1¼ teaspoons unflavored gelatin

3 large egg yolks

3 tablespoons honey

1 teaspoon pure vanilla extract

Whipped Coconut Cream for topping (see recipe in Chapter 10)

Optional: Banana slices and toasted coconut for decorating

1. Mash half of a banana to baby food consistency and measure out ¼ cup.

2. In a small saucepan, add the can of coconut milk and coconut butter. Sprinkle the gelatin on the top of the milk. Allow the gelatin to bloom (soften) about 5–10 minutes.

3. Meanwhile, in a small bowl, whisk together the egg yolks, honey, and vanilla. Set aside.

4. Once gelatin has softened, place saucepan over medium heat. Add the mashed banana and whisk constantly until well combined and the milk is warmed.

5. Very slowly add ½ cup of the warm milk to the yolks, whisking constantly to combine. Slowly pour the yolk mixture into the saucepan and whisk thoroughly.

6. Bring the mixture to a gentle simmer and whisk for 2–3 minutes until slightly thickened. Then pour the custard through a fine mesh strainer into a shallow dish to cool.

7. Once cooled, cover with plastic wrap pressed right against the pastry cream. (This will prevent a thick skin from forming on the surface.)

8. Refrigerate for at least 8 hours, preferably overnight. Once pastry cream is cold and set, whisk gently to loosen, so it's thick and creamy like custard. Set aside.

9. Remove the chilled tart crust from the fridge. Thinly slice the remaining bananas and layer them in 2 stacks along the bottom of the tart crust.

10. Spoon the custard over the banana layer and use an offset spatula to even out the top. Carefully remove the side of the tart pan and transfer the tart to a serving plate or cake stand. Top with fresh Whipped Coconut Cream. For a decorative touch, add sliced bananas and toasted coconut, if desired. Serve immediately, or refrigerate for up to 12 hours.

Favorite Fruit Tart

Makes 8 Servings

My adoration for pastry cream paired with fresh summer berries is best showcased in this exquisite masterpiece that combines the two within a delicate pastry crust. This light, refreshing dessert is as delectable as it is beautiful. It's also very versatile, since you can use whatever berries are in season.

1 Honey Graham Crust, chilled (see recipe in this chapter)

1 (13.5-ounce) can of pure coconut milk (1¾ cups)

1 teaspoon coconut butter

1¼ teaspoons unflavored gelatin

3 large egg yolks

3 tablespoons honey

1 teaspoon pure vanilla extract

3 cups seasonal berries

1. In a small saucepan, add the can of coconut milk and coconut butter. Sprinkle the gelatin on the top of the milk. Allow the gelatin to bloom (soften) about 5–10 minutes.

2. Meanwhile, in a small bowl, whisk together the egg yolks, honey, and vanilla. Set aside.

3. Once gelatin has softened, place saucepan over medium heat. Whisk constantly until the milk and gelatin are well combined and the milk is warmed.

4. Very slowly add ½ cup of the warm milk to the yolks, whisking constantly to combine. Slowly pour the yolk mixture into the saucepan and whisk thoroughly.

5. Bring the mixture to a gentle simmer and whisk for 2–3 minutes until slightly thickened. Then pour the custard through a fine mesh strainer into a shallow dish to cool.

6. Once cooled, cover with plastic wrap pressed right against the pastry cream. (This will prevent a thick skin from forming on the surface.) Refrigerate for at least 8 hours, preferably overnight. Once pastry cream is cold and set, whisk gently to loosen, so it's thick and creamy like custard.

7. Spoon the custard into the chilled tart crust and use an offset spatula to even out the top. Carefully remove the side of the tart pan and transfer the tart to a serving plate or cake stand. Arrange the fresh berries in a pleasing pattern across the top. Serve immediately, or refrigerate for up to 12 hours.

Peachy Raspberry Crisp

Makes 4–5 Servings

Growing up in the South, one of the highlights of summer was enjoying fresh, sweet, and juicy seasonal peaches. If you share my affinity for these little fuzzy treats, a great idea is to purchase a couple of crates each summer when they're in season. That way, you can slice and freeze them for use all year long for special favorites like this scrumptious Peachy Raspberry Crisp.

FILLING

¼ cup pure apple juice (or orange juice)

¼ teaspoon unflavored gelatin

1 tablespoon honey

1 teaspoon vanilla

⅛ teaspoon ground cinnamon

4 ripe medium peaches, peeled and sliced (or 4 cups frozen peach slices, thawed)

1 cup raspberries

TOPPING

1 cup blanched almond flour

⅓ cup sliced almonds

3 tablespoons unsalted butter or coconut oil, melted

1 tablespoon honey

⅛ teaspoon ground cinnamon

Pinch of sea salt

Optional: Vanilla Bean Frozen Yogurt for topping (see recipe in Chapter 10)

1. Preheat oven to 350°F. Lightly oil the bottom and sides of an 8" × 8" baking dish.

2. **For the Filling:** In a large bowl, add juice and sprinkle gelatin over the top. Allow it to sit about 5 minutes to soften. Then whisk in the honey, vanilla, and cinnamon.

3. Add the peach slices and raspberries to the honey mixture and toss to thoroughly coat. Transfer to prepared 8" × 8" baking dish.

4. **For the Topping:** In a medium bowl, combine the topping ingredients— blanched almond flour, sliced almonds, melted butter (or coconut oil), honey, cinnamon, and salt.

5. Spoon (or use hands to crumble) the topping evenly over the peaches and raspberries.

6. Bake approximately 20–22 minutes, until topping is golden brown. Allow to cool about 5 minutes before serving.

7. For an extra special treat, top with a scoop of homemade Vanilla Bean Frozen Yogurt and drizzle with the peach-berry sauce at the bottom of the baking dish. Enjoy!

Recipe Variation

For a delicious wintertime treat, use thinly sliced pears and fresh cranberries in place of the peaches and raspberries.

Apple Cinnamon Crisp

Makes 4–5 Servings

I adore the sweet smell of hot apple crisp baking in the oven—there is something so heartwarming and cozy about it! This healthier grain-free version is naturally sweetened with just a touch of honey, so you can enjoy the full, rich flavor of baked apples in every bite!

BAKED APPLES

¼ cup pure apple juice

¼ teaspoon unflavored gelatin

1 tablespoon honey

1½ teaspoons ground cinnamon

1 teaspoon vanilla

5 medium apples, cored and sliced

CRISP TOPPING

1 cup blanched almond flour

⅓ cup sliced blanched almonds

3 tablespoons unsalted butter (or coconut oil), melted

1 tablespoon honey

¼ teaspoon ground cinnamon

Pinch of sea salt

Optional: Vanilla Bean Frozen Yogurt for topping (see recipe in Chapter 10)

1. Preheat oven to 375°F. Lightly oil the bottom and sides of an 9" × 9" baking dish.

2. **For the Baked Apples:** In a large bowl, add juice and sprinkle gelatin over the top. Allow it to sit about 5 minutes to soften. Then whisk in the honey, cinnamon, and vanilla.

3. Add the apple slices to the honey mixture and toss to thoroughly coat. Transfer to prepared baking dish. Cover with foil and bake for 20 minutes.

4. **For the Crisp Topping:** While the apples are baking, in a medium bowl combine all of the topping ingredients.

5. When the apples have baked for 20 minutes, remove from oven. Spoon (or use hands to crumble) the topping over the apples.

6. Reduce oven temperature to 350°F. Place apple crisp in oven (uncovered) and continue baking about 15–18 minutes, until topping is golden brown. Allow to cool about 5 minutes before serving.

7. For an extra special treat, top with a scoop of homemade Vanilla Bean Frozen Yogurt and drizzle with the caramel-apple-like sauce at the bottom of the baking dish.

Basic Pie Crust

Makes 1 Pie Crust

Pie crusts are often the cause of much trepidation in the world of baking. But have no fear—this simple everyday pie crust comes together easily and is amazingly flaky and tender, despite the fact that it's grain-free.

2¼ cups blanched almond flour

1 tablespoon coconut flour

¼ teaspoon unflavored gelatin

¼ teaspoon sea salt

3 tablespoons palm shortening

1 tablespoon honey

1 large egg white

1. In a food processor, combine the almond flour, coconut flour, gelatin, and salt. Pulse in the palm shortening until it's well incorporated. If you don't have a food processor, use a pastry cutter (or 2 knives) to cut the shortening into the flour.

2. Add the honey and egg white and pulse until a dough ball forms.

3. Carefully remove the dough and flatten it into a small disk. Wrap in plastic and place it in the fridge to chill for 20–30 minutes.

4. Preheat oven to 325°F. Lightly oil a 9" pie dish with palm shortening.

5. Once dough is chilled, remove it from the fridge and place it into the prepared pie dish.

6. Starting with the sides of the dish, break off small pieces of dough and use your fingers to press them along the edge of the dish to form a sturdy crust. Press the remaining dough evenly along the bottom of the dish to connect the bottom and sides together.

7. Poke the bottom of the crust with a fork and bake 12–14 minutes until crust is golden brown. Allow the crust to cool and then fill it as desired.

Crispy Grain-Free Granola

Makes 5–6 Cups

One crunchy bite is all it takes to become completely smitten with this simple grain-free granola. Its slightly sweet cinnamony flavor with rich vanilla undertones combines beautifully with crisp toasted coconut and your favorite fresh or dried fruit. It's perfect with a splash of almond milk, or as a topping for yogurt parfaits.

NUT MIXTURE

1½ cups raw whole almonds

1 cup raw whole cashews

1 cup raw walnut halves

1 teaspoon sea salt

ALL-NATURAL SWEETENER

¼ cup coconut butter, softened

½ cup honey

2 tablespoons pure vanilla extract

1 tablespoon ground cinnamon

1 teaspoon coconut flour

¼ teaspoon sea salt

ADD-INS

¾ cup unsweetened coconut flakes

Your favorite fresh or dried fruit

1. **For the Nut Mixture:** Place the nuts and salt in a large bowl and cover with warm filtered water. Cover the bowl with a plate or clean kitchen towel, and allow the nuts to soak 18–24 hours.

2. When soaking time is completed, drain and rinse nuts. Place on a clean kitchen towel to absorb excess moisture.

3. **For the All-Natural Sweetener:** In a large bowl, whisk together the softened coconut butter and honey until smooth and creamy. Then add the remaining ingredients (vanilla, cinnamon, coconut flour, and salt). Whisk until well combined; set aside.

4. **For the Granola:** Preheat oven to 210°F. Line a 12" × 17" rimmed baking sheet with parchment paper. Set aside.

5. Using a food processor, place a couple of handfuls of the soaked nuts into the processor bowl and pulse to chop the nuts until they are about the size of oats. (Do not overprocess or you will create nut meal.)

6. Add the finely chopped nuts to the bowl with the honey mixture. Continue to pulse the whole nuts a few handfuls at a time until finished and continue adding them to the bowl with the honey mixture. Once all the nuts are ground, use a rubber spatula to fold them into the honey mixture until well combined.

7. Spoon the granola mixture onto the parchment-lined baking sheet. Use an offset spatula to evenly spread the granola across the pan into a thin layer. Bake the granola for 2 hours, then remove from the oven and gently flip section by section using a spatula, making sure to separate any large pieces into small cereal clusters.

8. Return granola to the oven and bake another 2 hours. Then repeat the process of gently flipping the granola. Sprinkle top with unsweetened coconut flakes.

9. Return granola to the oven again and bake another 30–45 minutes, just until the coconut is slightly toasted.

10. Turn off the oven. Place the baking sheet of granola on the stovetop to cool. After about 5–8 minutes, check the granola for the crunch-factor. If it's crunchy enough for you, allow it to continue cooling. If it isn't crunchy enough, return it to the warm oven and allow it to sit in the warm oven for 20–30 minutes more until it reaches desired level of crispness. Allow the granola to completely cool for about 45 minutes, then immediately transfer it to mason jars, or other airtight containers.

11. Store in the pantry for up to 2 weeks or in the fridge for about 3 weeks, or the freezer for up to 3 months. Enjoy with your favorite add-ins such as fresh or dried fruit.

Tips & Tidbits

It's common for raw nuts to change color when soaked together. Don't worry, no one will notice any unusual hues once the nuts have been ground, mixed with sweetener, and baked.

Honey Graham Crust

Makes 1 Tart Crust

The secret to flaky grain-free pie crusts is unflavored gelatin, since it helps to bind gluten-free ingredients together and helps the crust better hold up to moist fillings. That's why this slightly chewy, cookie-like crust is perfect for creamy chilled desserts like my decadent Banana Cream Tart or Favorite Fruit Tart (see recipes in this chapter).

2 cups blanched almond flour

2 tablespoons coconut flour

¼ teaspoon unflavored gelatin

¼ teaspoon sea salt

6 tablespoons palm shortening

2 tablespoons honey

1 teaspoon cold water

1. In a food processor, combine the almond flour, coconut flour, gelatin, and salt. Pulse in the palm shortening until it's well incorporated. If you don't have a food processor, use a pastry cutter (or 2 knives) to cut the shortening into the flour.

2. Add the honey and water and pulse until a dough ball forms.

3. Carefully remove the dough and flatten it into a small disk. Wrap in plastic and place it in the fridge to chill for 20–30 minutes.

4. Preheat oven to 325°F. Lightly oil a 9" tart pan with palm shortening. Trace the bottom of the tart pan on a sheet of parchment paper and trim it out slightly smaller so it fits into the bottom of the tart pan.

5. Once dough is chilled, remove it from the fridge and place it into the parchment-lined tart pan.

6. Starting with the sides of the dish, break off small pieces of dough and use your fingers to press them along the edge of the dish to form a sturdy crust. Press the remaining dough evenly along the bottom of the pan to connect the bottom and sides together.

7. Poke the bottom of the crust with a fork. Place the tart pan on a baking sheet and bake 12–14 minutes until crust is golden brown. Carefully remove it from the oven and allow the crust to cool, then fill it as desired.

Chocolate Graham Crust

Makes 1 Tart Crust

A decadent spin on my Honey Graham Crust (see recipe in this chapter), this rich chocolate version uses unsweetened cocoa powder to satisfy those who enjoy decadent chocolate treats. This crust is perfect for making a delightful Double Chocolate Cream Pie, or use it to create a luscious chocolate variation of my Banana Cream Tart (see recipes in this chapter).

1¾ cups blanched almond flour

3 tablespoons unsweetened cocoa powder

2 tablespoons coconut flour

¼ teaspoon unflavored gelatin

¼ teaspoon sea salt

5 tablespoons palm shortening

3 tablespoons honey

1. In a food processor, combine the almond flour, cocoa powder, coconut flour, gelatin, and salt. Pulse in the palm shortening until it's well incorporated. If you don't have a food processor, use a pastry cutter (or 2 knives) to cut the shortening into the flour.

2. Add the honey and pulse until a dough ball forms.

3. Carefully remove the dough and flatten it into a small disk. Wrap in plastic and place it in the fridge to chill for 20–30 minutes.

4. Preheat oven to 325°F. Lightly oil a 9" tart pan with palm shortening. Trace the bottom of the tart pan on a sheet of parchment paper and trim it out slightly smaller so it fits into the bottom of the tart pan.

5. Once dough is chilled, remove it from the fridge and place it into the parchment-lined tart pan.

6. Starting with the sides of the dish, break off small pieces of dough and use your fingers to press them along the edge of the dish to form a sturdy crust. Press the remaining dough evenly along the bottom of the pan to connect the bottom and sides together.

7. Poke the bottom of the crust with a fork. Place the tart pan on a baking sheet and bake 12–14 minutes until crust is golden brown. Carefully remove it from the oven and allow the crust to cool, then fill it as desired.

Chapter

7

CAKES AND CUPCAKES

Chocolate-Lovers' Cupcakes (DFO)

Strawberry Vanilla Custard Cake (DFO) (SCD)

Lemonade Sunshine Cake (DFO) (SCD)

Happy, Happy Ice Cream Cake (DFO)

Boston Cream Pie (DFO)

Pumpkin Praline Bundt Cake (DF) (SCD)

Cinnamon Crumb Coffee Cake (DFO) (SCD)

Very Vanilla Cupcakes (DFO) (SCD)

Little Lemon Cupcakes (DFO) (NF) (SCD)

Vanilla Layer Cake (DFO) (SCD)

Chocolate Layer Cake (DFO)

Apple Streusel Cake (DFO) (SCD)

Pumpkin Spice Cake (DF) (SCD)

Chocolate-Lovers' Cupcakes

(DFO)

Makes 10 Cupcakes

This delightful chocolate treat is the result of my passion for developing a true cakelike confection that makes you feel like you're not missing out on one of life's simplest of pleasures. With its rich chocolate flavor and moist light texture, this little treat is one of my treasured favorites and is sure to become one of yours, too.

1¾ cups blanched almond flour

1 tablespoon coconut flour

1 tablespoon, plus 1 teaspoon unsweetened cocoa powder

½ teaspoon baking soda

¼ teaspoon salt

¼ cup dairy-free mini chocolate chips

⅓ cup honey

2 tablespoons unsalted butter (or palm shortening)

2 tablespoons pure coconut milk

1 teaspoon pure vanilla extract

1 teaspoon apple cider vinegar

2 large eggs, plus 1 egg white

1. Preheat oven to 325°F. Place 10 parchment muffin liners into a 12-cup muffin tin; set aside.

2. In a food processor, combine the almond flour, coconut flour, unsweetened cocoa powder, baking soda, and salt.

3. In a medium saucepan, add all of the remaining ingredients except the eggs and egg white. Warm them over low heat, whisking the ingredients together until the chocolate is melted and everything is well incorporated.

4. Transfer the chocolate mixture to the food processor, using a rubber spatula to help scrape out all of the chocolate from the pan.

5. Cover and pulse a few times to combine. Then process until the batter is smooth and creamy (about 25–30 seconds).

6. Add the eggs and egg white. Cover and pulse a few times to combine. Then process just enough to blend the eggs into the batter (about 10–15 seconds). Use a thin spatula to scrape down the sides as needed.

7. Carefully spoon the cupcake batter into the lined muffin cups. Lightly tap the muffin tin on a kitchen towel on the counter to even out the tops.

8. Bake 18–20 minutes until light golden brown along edges and a toothpick inserted into center comes out clean. Allow cupcakes to cool in muffin tin about 5 minutes, then transfer to a wire rack to finish cooling. Top with your favorite frosting from Chapter 10 and enjoy!

Strawberry Vanilla Custard Cake

Makes 8 Servings

Light and refreshing, this beautiful strawberry layer cake is as simple to make as it is delicious. The cake and custard can be prepared a day in advance, making it easy to put this delightful confection together for a special occasion, or just because.

2 8" vanilla cakes, refrigerated (see Vanilla Layer Cake recipe in this chapter)

1 cup Lemon Curd, chilled (see recipe in Chapter 10)

2 (13.5-ounce) cans of coconut milk, refrigerated overnight (or 1 (14-ounce) can of pure coconut cream, chilled)

2–3 teaspoons honey

1 pint fresh strawberries, hulled and halved

1. Place your stand mixer bowl (or large mixing bowl) into the freezer, along with the whisk attachment (or beaters). Allow them to chill for a few minutes.

2. Remove the cold coconut cream from the 2 cans of cold coconut milk and place into the chilled mixing bowl. An easy way to do this is to open the cans from the bottom and carefully pour off the coconut water into a small mason jar for another use. This makes it easier to scoop out just the coconut cream. Or you can use pure coconut cream instead, which does not require removing the coconut water.

3. Attach the whisk (or beaters if using an electric hand mixer) and mix on high for 3–5 minutes until the coconut cream is light and fluffy. Add 2–3 teaspoons of honey and continue to whisk until well incorporated.

4. Measure out 1 cup of Lemon Curd and spoon it into the whipped coconut cream. Mix on low to incorporate. Then increase to high and whip the mixture until it's light and fluffy. Cover and place in fridge to set.

5. When ready to assemble the cake, remove the cakes from the fridge. Place one cake on a cake stand and spoon half of the whipped lemon curd on top of the cake. Place the second cake on top and press slightly to secure.

6. Frost the top only of the second cake with the remaining whipped lemon curd topping. Place the berry halves along the border of the cake for an elegant touch.

7. Refrigerate for 1 hour and then serve. Or the cake may be refrigerated for up to 12 hours before serving.

Tips & Tidbits

I recommend making the cakes and the Lemon Curd the day before you plan to serve this cake. Doing so will make it much easier to quickly put the cake together.

Lemonade Sunshine Cake

Makes 8 Servings

I'm an unabashed romantic, and as such, I find it deeply rewarding when I can create a recipe that stirs the heart. This luscious lemon cake with its velvety-smooth texture and rich lemony flavor brings such delight that even the most composed individuals have found themselves eagerly savoring a second slice.

FILLING AND FROSTING

1 batch of Lemon Curd (see recipe in Chapter 10)

1 batch of Creamy Lemon Frosting, chilled (see recipe in Chapter 10)

CAKE

3½ cups blanched almond flour

¼ cup coconut flour

1 teaspoon baking soda

½ teaspoon salt

3 tablespoons plain Whole Milk Yogurt or Coconut Milk Yogurt (see recipes in Chapter 10)

½ cup honey

3 tablespoons unsalted butter, melted, (or palm shortening)

½ cup pure coconut milk

2 tablespoons pure vanilla extract

2 teaspoons apple cider vinegar

4 large eggs, plus 2 egg whites

1. **For the Filling and Frosting:** A day or two before you plan to bake this cake, make the Lemon Curd. Cover and refrigerate. Once the Lemon Curd is completely chilled, measure out ¾ cup and use it to make the Creamy Lemon Frosting. Reserve the remaining Lemon Curd for use as the filling for the cake layers.

2. **For the Cake:** Preheat oven to 325°F. Lightly oil 2 6" cake pans. Trace the bottom of the pans on a sheet of parchment paper and trim them out slightly smaller so they fit into the bottom of the cake pans.

3. In a food processor, combine the almond flour, coconut flour, baking soda, and salt.

4. Add all of the remaining ingredients except the eggs and egg whites to the top of the dry ingredients in the order given.

5. Cover and pulse a few times to combine. Then process until the batter is smooth and creamy (about 25–30 seconds).

6. Add the eggs and egg whites. Cover and pulse a few times to combine. Then process just enough to blend the eggs into the batter (about 10–15 seconds). Use a thin spatula as needed to scrape down the sides.

7. Divide the cake batter evenly between the 2 cake pans. Use an offset spatula to smooth out the tops.

8. Bake the cakes for about 35–40 minutes until light golden brown along edges and a toothpick inserted into center comes out clean. Allow the cakes to cool on the stovetop about 5 minutes, then invert each cake onto a plate. Remove the parchment liner and use an additional plate to invert each cake right-side up onto its own plate.

9. Allow the cakes to cool to room temperature. Cover and refrigerate until they're completely chilled. Remove the cakes from the fridge and carefully cut the 2 cakes in half horizontally to form 4 layers.

10. Begin to assemble by placing 1 dome layer face down on a cake plate. Spread ⅓ of the remaining Lemon Curd across the top. Add another cake layer, pressing it slightly into the lemon curd to secure it in place. Repeat the process of adding Lemon Curd to each layer until you add the final layer to the cake.

11. Remove the Creamy Lemon Frosting from the fridge; allow to sit for 5 minutes if too firm to spread. Then use a large offset cake spatula to frost the top and sides of the cake. Decorate using lemon slices and edible flowers, if desired.

12. Refrigerate for 1 hour and then serve. Or the cake may be refrigerated for up to 12 hours before serving.

Tips & Tidbits

You can make this delectable cake using 2 8" cake pans as well. Just adjust the bake time to 28–30 minutes. The layers will be a bit thinner than with the smaller 6" pan, but the cake will taste just as delicious!

Happy, Happy Ice Cream Cake

(DFO)

Makes 12 Servings

Whatever the happy occasion, this decadent ice cream cake is certain to put a big smile on your favorite faces! That's why any time we've got a special something to celebrate, this is one of our favorite go-to desserts. It's certain to make any occasion an even happier one!

TOPPING

1 quart of homemade Vanilla Bean Frozen Yogurt (see recipe in Chapter 10)

1½ cups diced fresh cherries

¾ cup dairy-free mini chocolate chips

CAKE

3½ cups blanched almond flour

2 tablespoons coconut flour

3 tablespoons unsweetened cocoa powder

1 teaspoon baking soda

½ teaspoon salt

½ cup dairy-free mini chocolate chips

⅔ cup honey

3 tablespoons unsalted butter (or palm shortening)

¼ cup pure coconut milk

2 teaspoons pure vanilla extract

2 teaspoons apple cider vinegar

4 large eggs, plus 2 egg whites

1. **For the Topping:** A day or two ahead of time, make the Vanilla Bean Frozen Yogurt and fold in the diced cherries and chocolate chips. Place in freezer to harden.

2. **For the Cake:** Preheat oven to 325°F. Lightly oil a 9" × 13" baking dish with palm shortening.

3. In a food processor, combine the almond flour, coconut flour, unsweetened cocoa powder, baking soda, and salt.

4. In a medium saucepan, add all of the remaining ingredients except the eggs and egg white. Warm them over low heat, whisking the ingredients together until the chocolate is melted and everything is well incorporated.

5. Transfer the chocolate mixture to the food processor, using a rubber spatula to help scrape out all of the chocolate from the pan.

6. Cover and pulse a few times to combine. Then process until the batter is smooth and creamy (about 25–30 seconds).

7. Add the eggs and egg whites. Cover and pulse a few times to combine. Then process just enough to blend the eggs into the batter (about 10–15 seconds). Use a thin spatula as needed to scrape down the sides.

8. Pour the cake batter evenly into the prepared baking dish. Use an offset spatula to smooth out the top.

9. Bake the cake for 30–32 minutes until light golden brown along edges and a toothpick inserted into center comes out clean. Allow the cake to cool on the stovetop about 30 minutes. Place in the fridge to finish chilling completely.

10. When ready to assemble, take the frozen yogurt out of the freezer to allow it to soften. Then scoop it over the cake and use an offset spatula to evenly distribute the frozen yogurt across the top of the cake. Cover the cake and place it in the freezer to harden, or until you're ready to serve.

11. About 15 minutes before you plan to serve the cake, take it out of the freezer to allow the cake and ice cream to soften a bit so it's easier to slice.

Boston Cream Pie

(DFO)

Makes 8 Servings

Technically not a pie, this classic confection is named after its birthplace. Personally, I'm not too concerned with the details surrounding the origins of its name; it's the unbelievably decadent taste that leads me to say with carefree abandon: Let us eat cake, or pie, or whatever it's called! After just one bite, I'm certain you'll feel the same way.

2 8" vanilla cakes, chilled (see Vanilla Layer Cake recipe in this chapter)

1 (13.5-ounce) can of pure coconut milk (1¾ cups)

1 teaspoon coconut butter

1¼ teaspoons unflavored gelatin

3 large egg yolks

3 tablespoons honey

1 teaspoon pure vanilla extract

1 batch of Chocolate Ganache icing (see recipe in Chapter 10)

1. In a small saucepan, add the can of coconut milk and coconut butter. Sprinkle the gelatin on the top of the milk. Allow the gelatin to bloom (soften) about 5–10 minutes.

2. Meanwhile, in a small bowl, whisk together the egg yolks, honey, and vanilla. Set aside.

3. Once gelatin has softened, place saucepan over medium heat. Whisk constantly until the milk and gelatin are well combined and the milk is warmed.

4. Slowly add ½ cup of the warm milk to the yolks, whisking constantly to combine. Then pour the yolk mixture into the saucepan and whisk thoroughly.

5. Bring the mixture to a gentle simmer and whisk for 2–3 minutes until slightly thickened. Pour the custard through a fine mesh strainer into a shallow dish to cool.

6. Once cooled, cover with plastic wrap pressed right against the pastry cream. (This will prevent a thick skin from forming on the surface.)

7. Refrigerate for at least 8 hours, preferably overnight. Once pastry cream is cold and set, whisk gently to loosen, so it's thick and creamy like custard.

8. On the day you plan to serve the cake, make the Chocolate Ganache and allow it to sit about 1–2 hours at room temperature to cool. When the Ganache has cooled, remove the cakes and pastry cream from the fridge. Place one cake on a cake stand and spoon the pastry cream over the top. Place the second cake on top and press slightly to secure.

9. Frost the top of the cake with the cooled Chocolate Ganache icing. Refrigerate for 1 hour and then serve. Or the cake may be refrigerated for up to 12 hours before serving.

Tips & Tidbits

I recommend making the cakes and the pastry cream a day or two in advance. It makes it much easier to quickly put the cake together when you're ready to serve.

Pumpkin Praline Bundt Cake

Makes 8–10 Servings

Hosting an afternoon tea is an easy, thoughtful way to gather with friends to catch up on each other's lives, or to celebrate a special occasion. This simple, pretty bundt cake is a favorite of mine for fall entertaining. It's perfect paired with an assortment of herbal teas and tisanes.

PRALINE CENTER

1 tablespoon coconut oil, melted

2 tablespoons honey

1 teaspoon ground cinnamon

½ cup pecan pieces

CAKE

3 cups blanched almond flour

2 tablespoons coconut flour

1 teaspoon baking soda

½ teaspoon sea salt

¼ cup coconut oil

½ cup honey

⅓ cup coconut milk

¾ cup pumpkin purée

1 tablespoon pure vanilla extract

2 teaspoons Pumpkin Pie Spice (see recipe in Chapter 10)

1 teaspoon apple cider vinegar

3 large eggs, plus 2 egg whites

Optional: Unsweetened shredded coconut for topping the cake

1. Preheat oven to 340°F. Generously oil a 10" bundt pan; set aside.

2. **For the Praline Center:** In a small bowl, whisk together the coconut oil, honey, and cinnamon. Add the pecans and toss well to coat. Set aside.

3. **For the Cake:** In a food processor, combine the almond flour, coconut flour, baking soda, and salt. Add all of the remaining ingredients except the eggs and egg whites to the top of the dry ingredients in the order given.

4. Cover and pulse a few times to combine. Then process until the batter is smooth and creamy (about 25–30 seconds).

5. Add the eggs and egg whites. Cover and pulse a few times to combine. Then process just enough to blend the eggs into the batter (about 10–15 seconds). Use a thin spatula as needed to scrape down the sides.

6. Carefully spoon half of the batter into the prepared bundt pan. Spoon the praline filling around the center of the bundt pan, trying not to get it too close to the edges. Spoon the remaining cake batter on top of the praline. Use the back of a spoon to smooth the top, as needed.

7. Bake for approximately 35–38 minutes until slightly golden brown around the edges and a toothpick inserted into center comes out clean. Allow the cake to cool on the stovetop about 5 minutes. Then invert it onto a cake stand or serving plate. Sprinkle top with unsweetened coconut, if desired.

Cinnamon Crumb Coffee Cake

Makes 9 Servings

I cannot think of a better accompaniment to a cup of coffee or tea than a scrumptious, grain-free coffee cake filled with a gooey cinnamon center and crunchy crumb topping. The sweet aroma of this cake baking combined with the scent of freshly brewed coffee is simply irresistible!

TOPPING

1 tablespoon butter (or coconut oil)

1 tablespoon, plus 1 teaspoon honey

1½ teaspoons ground cinnamon

1 cup walnut pieces, finely chopped

CINNAMON SWIRL

1 tablespoon unsalted butter (or coconut oil)

2 tablespoons honey

1 tablespoon ground cinnamon

CAKE

3½ cups blanched almond flour

¼ cup coconut flour

1 teaspoon baking soda

½ teaspoon salt

½ cup honey

¼ cup unsalted butter, melted, (or palm shortening)

½ cup pure coconut milk

1 tablespoon pure vanilla extract

2 teaspoons apple cider vinegar

4 large eggs, plus 2 egg whites

1. Preheat oven to 315°F. Lightly oil a 9" × 9" baking dish; set aside.

2. **For the Topping:** In a small bowl, whisk together the butter (or coconut oil), honey, and cinnamon until well blended. Add the finely chopped walnuts and toss well to combine. Set aside.

3. **For the Cinnamon Swirl:** In a small bowl, whisk together the butter (or coconut oil), honey, and cinnamon until well blended. Set aside.

4. **For the Cake:** In a food processor, combine the almond flour, coconut flour, baking soda, and salt. Add all of the remaining ingredients except the eggs and egg whites to the top of the dry ingredients in the order given. Cover and pulse a few times to combine. Then process until the batter is smooth and creamy (about 20–25 seconds).

5. Add the eggs and egg whites. Cover and pulse a few times to combine. Then process just enough to blend the eggs into the batter (about 10–15 seconds). Use a thin spatula as needed to scrape down the sides.

6. Carefully spoon half of the batter into the prepared baking dish. Use an offset spatula to smooth out the top.

7. Drizzle with the cinnamon swirl across the top of the batter. Then carefully spoon the remaining cake batter on top. Use an offset spatula to smooth the top of the batter. Next, starting at the edges of the cake, crumble the topping evenly across the cake. Use your fingers to gently press the topping into the batter a bit.

8. Bake the cake for 45–55 minutes until light golden brown along edges and a toothpick inserted into center comes out clean. Allow the cake to cool on the stovetop about 5 minutes. Serve warm with your favorite coffee or tea.

Very Vanilla Cupcakes

(DFO) (SCD)

Makes 10 Cupcakes

It's an amazing tale of cupcake-baking adventures that led to that "Eureka!" moment when this recipe finally came together. If you've tried many of the grain-free cupcake recipes out there and been disappointed, you will be especially delighted to discover this light and moist—truly cakelike—treat. It's one of my favorite new recipes because everyone deserves to enjoy a truly scrumptious cupcake!

1¾ cups blanched almond flour

2 tablespoons coconut flour

½ teaspoon baking soda

¼ teaspoon salt

1 tablespoon plain Whole Milk Yogurt or Coconut Milk Yogurt (see recipes in Chapter 10)

¼ cup honey

1 tablespoon unsalted butter, melted (or palm shortening)

¼ cup pure coconut milk

1 tablespoon pure vanilla extract

1 teaspoon apple cider vinegar

2 large eggs, plus 1 egg white

1. Preheat oven to 325°F. Place 10 parchment muffin liners into a 12-cup muffin tin; set aside.

2. In a food processor, combine the almond flour, coconut flour, baking soda, and salt.

3. Add all of the remaining ingredients except the eggs and egg white to the top of the dry ingredients in the order given.

4. Cover and pulse a few times to combine. Then process until the batter is smooth and creamy (about 25–30 seconds).

5. Add the eggs and egg white. Cover and pulse a few times to combine. Then process just enough to blend the eggs into the batter (about 10–15 seconds). Use a thin spatula as needed to scrape down the sides.

6. Carefully spoon the cupcake batter into the lined muffin cups. Lightly tap the muffin tin on a kitchen towel on the counter to even out the tops.

7. Bake 18–20 minutes until light golden brown along edges and a toothpick inserted into center comes out clean. Allow cupcakes to cool in muffin tin about 5 minutes, then transfer to a wire rack to finish cooling.

8. Top with your favorite frosting from Chapter 10 and enjoy!

Little Lemon Cupcakes

Makes 24 Mini Cupcakes

The sweet, tangy flavor of these adorable little cupcakes is reminiscent of lemon drop candies. Top them with my simple Creamy Lemon Frosting and you have a delicious bite-sized treat that is perfect for any celebration!

½ cup coconut flour

½ teaspoon baking soda

¼ teaspoon sea salt

⅓ cup honey

3 tablespoons unsalted butter, melted, (or coconut oil)

4 large eggs

1 tablespoon lemon zest

¼ cup lemon juice

1 batch Creamy Lemon Frosting (see recipe in Chapter 10)

1. Preheat oven to 340°F. Place 24 parchment mini-muffin liners into a 24-cup mini-muffin tin; set aside.

2. In a small bowl, mix together the coconut flour, baking soda, and salt.

3. In a large bowl, whisk together the honey and butter (or coconut oil). Then whisk in the eggs, lemon zest, and lemon juice until well combined.

4. Add the dry ingredients to the wet and whisk well to thoroughly combine, until no lumps remain and batter begins to thicken.

5. Allow batter to sit 5 minutes so the coconut flour can absorb some of the liquid. Then evenly distribute the batter among the 24 mini-muffin cups.

6. Bake for approximately 20–24 minutes, until edges begin to turn a light golden brown and a toothpick inserted into center comes out clean. Remove from oven and allow cupcakes to cool in the pan for 5–10 minutes. Transfer to a wire rack to finish cooling. Frost with Creamy Lemon Frosting and enjoy!

Vanilla Layer Cake

Makes 8 Servings

With its moist, light texture and delicate vanilla flavor, this simple recipe makes a delightful birthday cake—or use it as a base for creating other scrumptious layer cakes, such as my Boston Cream Pie or Strawberry Vanilla Custard Cake (see recipes in this chapter).

3½ cups blanched almond flour

¼ cup coconut flour

1 teaspoon baking soda

½ teaspoon salt

3 tablespoons plain Whole Milk Yogurt or Coconut Milk Yogurt (see recipes in Chapter 10)

½ cup honey

3 tablespoons unsalted butter, melted, (or palm shortening)

½ cup pure coconut milk

2 tablespoons pure vanilla extract

2 teaspoons apple cider vinegar

4 large eggs, plus 2 egg whites

1. Preheat oven to 325°F. Lightly oil 2 8" cake pans. Trace the bottom of the pans on a sheet of parchment paper and trim slightly smaller so they fit into the bottom of the cake pans.

2. In a food processor, combine the almond flour, coconut flour, baking soda, and salt.

3. Add all of the remaining ingredients except the eggs and egg whites to the top of the dry ingredients in the order given.

4. Cover and pulse a few times to combine. Then process until the batter is smooth and creamy (about 25–30 seconds).

5. Add the eggs and egg whites. Cover and pulse a few times to combine. Then process just enough to blend the eggs into the batter (about 10–15 seconds). Use a thin spatula as needed to scrape down the sides.

6. Divide the cake batter evenly between the 2 cake pans. Use an offset spatula to smooth out the tops.

7. Bake the cakes for 28–30 minutes until light golden brown along edges and a toothpick inserted into center comes out clean. Allow the cakes to cool on the stovetop about 5 minutes, then invert each cake onto a plate. Remove the parchment liner and use an additional plate to invert each cake right-side up onto its own plate.

8. Allow the cakes to cool completely, then frost them with your favorite frosting from Chapter 10 and enjoy!

Chocolate Layer Cake

(DFO)

Makes 8 Servings

Chocolate cake is not something to be taken lightly. It should be moist and rich with a decadent chocolate taste that satisfies even the most discriminating chocolate connoisseur. This simple recipe embodies all of that, and then some. In fact, it's so delectable no one will ever know it's grain-free!

3½ cups blanched almond flour

2 tablespoons coconut flour

3 tablespoons unsweetened cocoa powder

1 teaspoon baking soda

½ teaspoon salt

½ cup dairy-free mini chocolate chips

⅔ cup honey

3 tablespoons unsalted butter (or palm shortening)

¼ cup pure coconut milk

2 teaspoons pure vanilla extract

2 teaspoons apple cider vinegar

4 large eggs, plus 2 egg whites

Chocolate Cream Frosting (see recipe in Chapter 10)

1. Preheat oven to 325°F. Lightly oil 2 8" cake pans. Trace the bottom of the pans on a sheet of parchment paper and trim slightly smaller so they fit into the bottom of the cake pans.

2. In a food processor, combine the almond flour, coconut flour, unsweetened cocoa powder, baking soda, and salt.

3. In a medium saucepan, add all of the remaining ingredients except the eggs and egg white. Warm them over low heat, whisking the ingredients together until the chocolate is melted and everything is well incorporated.

4. Transfer the chocolate mixture to the food processor, using a rubber spatula to help scrape out all of the chocolate from the pan.

5. Cover and pulse a few times to combine. Then process until the batter is smooth and creamy (about 25–30 seconds).

6. Add the eggs and egg whites. Cover and pulse a few times to combine. Then process just enough to blend the eggs into the batter (about 10–15 seconds). Use a thin spatula as needed to scrape down the sides.

7. Divide the cake batter evenly between the 2 cake pans. Use an offset spatula to smooth out the tops.

8. Bake the cakes for 28–30 minutes until light golden brown along edges and a toothpick inserted into center comes out clean. Allow the cakes to cool on the stovetop about 5 minutes, then invert each cake onto a plate and remove the parchment liner.

9. Allow the cakes to cool completely, and then frost them with my decadent Chocolate Cream Frosting. Enjoy!

Tips & Tidbits

This cake recipe can also be used to make one 9" × 13" sheet cake. The bake time increases only slightly to about 30–32 minutes.

Apple Streusel Cake

Makes 8 Servings

Topped with a beautiful layer of cinnamon-apple goodness, this upside-down cake creates a lasting impression even before you take the first bite. This incredibly moist and delightful treat really captures the fabulous flavors of fall, which is why it always gets rave reviews!

APPLE TOPPING

1 medium apple

2 tablespoons unsalted butter (or coconut oil), melted

2 tablespoons maple syrup (or honey)

¼ teaspoon ground cinnamon

⅔ cup crispy walnut pieces

CAKE

2¼ cups blanched almond flour

1 teaspoon baking soda

½ teaspoon sea salt

1 teaspoon ground cinnamon

¼ teaspoon ground ginger

½ cup unsweetened applesauce

¼ cup maple syrup (or honey)

4 large eggs

1 teaspoon pure vanilla extract

1. Preheat oven to 350°F. Remove the bottom round of a 9" x 3" springform pan. Using parchment paper, trace the bottom round and cut the paper slightly smaller so that it fits neatly into the bottom. Place the bottom back into the springform pan and secure in place. Lightly oil the pan and then place the parchment cut-out into the bottom of the pan and lightly oil. (If you don't have a springform pan, you can use a parchment-lined 9" x 9" baking dish instead.)

2. **For the Apple Topping:** Core and slice 1 apple into ¼"-thick slices and arrange the apple slices in a pleasing pattern on the bottom of the prepared pan.

3. In a small bowl, combine the melted butter or coconut oil, maple syrup (or honey), and cinnamon. Toss the walnuts in the mixture until well coated.

4. Spoon the walnuts in a circular pattern across the top of the apple slices, filling in the gaps between the apple slices.

5. Place the pan in the oven and bake the topping for 6–8 minutes, just until the apples begin to soften. Then remove from oven and set aside.

6. **For the Cake:** While the topping is cooking, combine the almond flour, baking soda, salt, and spices in a small bowl. Set aside.

7. In a large mixing bowl, add the applesauce, maple syrup (or honey), eggs, and vanilla. Using a stand mixer or electric hand mixer, blend together until well combined.

8. Slowly mix the dry ingredients into the wet and continue mixing for a full minute, until smooth and well blended.

9. Gently pour the cake batter over the partially baked apple topping, using a rubber spatula to help remove all of the batter from the bowl. Spread batter evenly across top.

10. Place the cake back in oven and continue to bake for approximately 25–28 minutes, until a toothpick inserted into center comes out clean.

11. Allow cake to cool completely, then remove the springform pan and invert the cake onto a plate or cake stand to serve. (If using a 9" x 9" baking dish, place a serving platter over the top of the baking dish and invert the cake onto the platter.)

Pumpkin Spice Cake

Makes 8 Servings

I'm always looking for new ways to bring a tasty grain-free spin to old favorites, and this recipe brings together the familiar flavor of a rich spice cake with the moist texture and taste of pumpkin. No need for a reason to celebrate—this delightful cake is a special occasion in and of itself. Of course, a dollop or two of Whipped Coconut Cream makes a welcome accompaniment!

2¼ cups blanched almond flour

2 teaspoons Pumpkin Pie Spice (see recipe in Chapter 10)

1 teaspoon baking soda

½ teaspoon sea salt

1 cup pumpkin purée

½ cup honey

4 large eggs

½ teaspoon pure vanilla extract

Whipped Coconut Cream (see recipe in Chapter 10)

1. Preheat oven to 350°F. Remove the bottom round of a 9" × 3" springform pan. Using parchment paper, trace the bottom round and cut the paper slightly smaller so that it fits neatly into the bottom. Place the bottom back into the springform pan and secure in place. Lightly oil the pan and then place the parchment cut-out into the bottom of the pan and lightly oil it as well. (If you don't have a springform pan, you can use a parchment-lined 9" × 9" baking pan instead.)

2. In a small bowl, combine the almond flour, Pumpkin Pie Spice, baking soda, and salt. Set aside.

3. In a large mixing bowl, add the pumpkin purée, honey, eggs, and vanilla. Using a stand mixer or electric hand mixer, blend until well combined. Slowly add the dry ingredients into the wet and continue mixing for a full minute, until smooth and well blended.

4. Pour batter into prepared pan, making sure to even out the top.

5. Bake for approximately 25–28 minutes, until a toothpick inserted into center comes out clean. Allow cake to cool completely, then place in the fridge to chill.

6. If using a springform pan, remove the chilled cake from the pan and place on a cake stand. Frost the chilled cake with the Whipped Coconut Cream and serve immediately. Or refrigerate up to 12 hours before serving.

Chapter

8

CLASSIC COOKIES

Nutty Chocolate Chunk Cookies

(DFO) (EF)

Makes 1½ Dozen Cookies

This soft and chewy cookie with its chocolate chunks and crispy walnuts makes a wonderful treat on those special days when you just want a good cookie to share with your friends and family.

1¾ cups blanched almond flour

1 teaspoon coconut flour

¼ teaspoon baking soda

¼ scant teaspoon salt

2 tablespoons unsalted butter, softened, (or palm shortening)

2 tablespoons coconut oil

¼ cup honey

1 teaspoon vanilla extract

¼ cup walnut pieces

⅓ cup dairy-free chocolate chunks

1. Preheat oven to 350°F. Line a baking sheet with parchment paper. Set aside.

2. In a small bowl, combine the almond flour, coconut flour, baking soda, and salt.

3. In a large mixing bowl, mix together the butter (or palm shortening), coconut oil, honey, and vanilla. Using a stand mixer or electric hand mixer, blend together until smooth and creamy.

4. Add the dry ingredients to the wet and mix well to combine. Then, using a rubber spatula, fold in the walnut pieces and chocolate chunks.

5. Drop the dough by rounded spoonfuls at least 2" apart onto the parchment-lined baking sheet. Use your fingers to slightly flatten the cookies.

6. Bake for 8–10 minutes, until golden brown along edges. Allow the cookies to completely cool on the cookie sheet, as they will be very soft and crumbly when hot. Then transfer to a plate and serve.

Tips & Tidbits

These cookies are best served within an hour of baking, since almond flour cookies tend to soften as they sit at room temperature. However, a simple trick to re-crisp almond flour cookies is to reheat them on a parchment-lined baking sheet in a 195°F oven for about 4–6 minutes.

Snickerdoodles

Makes 1½ Dozen Cookies

Snickerdoodles are a scrumptious classic that no one should have to miss out on! After going grain-free, this was one of the first cookie recipes I just had to re-create for all of us cinnamon lovers to enjoy. They are delicious on their own, and even more of a treat when dipped in homemade almond milk.

COOKIES

2 cups blanched almond flour

1 teaspoon coconut flour

¼ teaspoon baking soda

¼ scant teaspoon salt

2 tablespoons unsalted butter, softened, (or palm shortening)

2 tablespoons coconut oil

¼ cup honey

1 tablespoon vanilla extract

TOPPING

2 teaspoons cinnamon

Optional: 1 tablespoon coconut crystals (omit for SCD)

1. **For the Cookies:** In a small bowl, combine the almond flour, coconut flour, baking soda, and salt.

2. In a large mixing bowl, add the butter (or palm shortening), coconut oil, honey, and vanilla. Using a stand mixer or electric hand mixer, blend together until smooth and creamy.

3. Add the dry ingredients to the wet and mix well to combine. Chill the dough for 30 minutes in the fridge.

4. **For the Topping:** Meanwhile, in a small bowl, mix together the cinnamon and coconut crystals (if using) for the topping. Set aside.

5. Preheat oven to 350°F. Line a baking sheet with parchment paper.

6. Once the dough is chilled, scoop out 1 rounded tablespoon and roll it into a ball. Then roll the dough ball into the cinnamon mixture until well coated on all sides. Repeat the process, placing the cinnamon-coated dough balls onto the parchment-lined baking sheet at least 2" apart. Use the palm of your hand, or the bottom of a small mason jar, to slightly flatten each cookie into a circle.

7. Bake for 8–10 minutes, until golden brown along edges. Allow the cookies to completely cool on the cookie sheet, as they will be very soft and crumbly when hot. Then transfer to a plate and serve with a tall glass of almond milk.

Almost Oatmeal Cookies

Makes 1½ Dozen Cookies

Unsweetened shredded coconut is the secret behind the chewy texture of this cookie, which is reminiscent of the oatmeal cookies many of us grew up enjoying. So grab a glass of almond milk and get ready for these delightful honey-sweetened treats!

1¼ cups blanched almond flour
1 teaspoon coconut flour
¼ teaspoon baking soda
⅛ teaspoon salt
2 tablespoons unsalted butter, softened, (or palm shortening)
2 tablespoons coconut oil
¼ cup honey
1 teaspoon vanilla extract
1¾ teaspoons ground cinnamon
½ cup unsweetened shredded coconut
⅓ cup organic raisins

1. Preheat oven to 350°F. Line a baking sheet with parchment paper. Set aside.

2. In a small bowl, combine the almond flour, coconut flour, baking soda, and salt.

3. In a large mixing bowl, add the butter (or palm shortening), coconut oil, honey, vanilla, and cinnamon. Using a stand mixer or electric hand mixer, blend together until smooth and creamy.

4. Add the dry ingredients to the wet and mix well to combine. Then add the shredded coconut, continuing to mix until well combined.

5. Using a rubber spatula, fold in the raisins. Then drop the dough by rounded spoonfuls at least 2" apart onto the parchment-lined baking sheet. Use your fingers to slightly flatten the cookies.

6. Bake for 8–10 minutes, until golden brown along edges. Allow the cookies to completely cool on the cookie sheet, as they will be very soft and crumbly when hot. Once cooled, they transform into the ultimate deliciously chewy treat!

Chocolate Ohs!

(DFO)

Makes 1 Dozen Sandwich Cookies

"Oh my, these are amazing!" is a common exclamation you'll hear when sharing these delightful little sandwich cookies with family and friends. That's why they're affectionately called Chocolate Ohs! Since options are always a good thing, you can choose to fill these special treats with either the luscious nut butter filling called for in the recipe or with The Best Cookie Icing recommended in the sidebar. Both are delicious!

NUT BUTTER FILLING

⅓ cup all-natural roasted nut butter of your choice
¼ cup honey
2–3 tablespoons coconut flour

COOKIES

1½ cups blanched almond flour
¼ teaspoon baking soda
¼ scant teaspoon sea salt
¼ cup unsalted butter, softened, (or palm shortening)
2 tablespoons coconut oil
½ cup, plus 1 tablespoon coconut crystals
¼ cup unsweetened cocoa powder
1 teaspoon pure vanilla extract
1 large egg white

1. **For the Nut Butter Filling:** Use a spoon to stir together the nut butter, honey, and coconut flour, starting with just 2 tablespoons of coconut flour. If the mixture doesn't form a stiff dough, continue to add 1 teaspoon of coconut flour at a time until the mixture comes together like cookie dough. Set aside.

2. **For the Cookies:** In a small bowl, combine the almond flour, baking soda, and salt.

3. In a large mixing bowl, add the butter (or palm shortening), coconut oil, coconut crystals, cocoa powder, and vanilla. Using a stand mixer or electric hand mixer, blend together until smooth and creamy. Then mix in the egg white until well incorporated.

4. Add the dry ingredients to the wet and mix well to combine. Chill the dough for 30 minutes in the fridge.

5. While the dough is chilling, preheat oven to 350°F. Line a baking sheet with parchment paper.

6. Once the dough is chilled, scoop out 1 rounded tablespoon and roll it into a ball. Place each dough ball onto the parchment-lined baking sheet at least 2" apart. Use the palm of your hand to slightly flatten each cookie into a circle.

7. Bake for 8–10 minutes, until lightly browned along edges. Allow the cookies to cool on the cookie sheet for 5 minutes, then transfer to a wire rack to finish cooling.

8. Once the cookies are completely cool, roll the nut butter filling into small dough balls and press each ball between 2 of the chocolate cookies to form a cookie sandwich. Enjoy immediately, or wrap individually and store in the fridge or freezer. Cookies will keep in fridge for 3–4 days and in freezer up to 1 month.

Recipe Variation
....

To create vanilla cream–filled cookie sandwiches, use The Best Cookie Icing to fill the cookies. (See recipe in Chapter 10.)

Ice Cream Cookie Sandwiches

(DFO) (EF) (SCD)

Makes 1 Dozen Cookie Sandwiches

Keep that ice cream man at bay with these tasty little Ice Cream Cookie Sandwiches. They not only taste great, but are a much healthier choice than commercial ice cream treats, since they're made with real-food ingredients and probiotic-rich homemade frozen vanilla yogurt.

1¾ cups blanched almond flour

1 teaspoon coconut flour

¼ teaspoon baking soda

¼ scant teaspoon salt

2 tablespoons unsalted butter, softened, (or palm shortening)

2 tablespoons coconut oil

¼ cup honey

1 teaspoon vanilla extract

¼ cup chopped dried cherries (or cranberries)

Optional: ¼ cup dairy-free mini chocolate chips (omit for SCD)

Vanilla Bean Frozen Yogurt (see recipe in Chapter 10)

1. Preheat oven to 350°F. Line a baking sheet with parchment paper. Set aside.

2. In a small bowl, combine the almond flour, coconut flour, baking soda, and salt.

3. In a large mixing bowl, add the butter (or palm shortening), coconut oil, honey, and vanilla. Using a stand mixer or electric hand mixer, blend together until smooth and creamy.

4. Add the dry ingredients to the wet and mix well to combine. Using a rubber spatula, fold in the dried cherries or cranberries, and chocolate chips, if desired.

5. Drop the dough by rounded spoonfuls at least 2" apart onto the parchment-lined baking sheet. Use your fingers to slightly flatten the cookies.

6. Bake for 8–10 minutes, until golden brown along edges. Allow the cookies to completely cool on the cookie sheet, as they will be very soft and crumbly when hot.

7. Once cooled, transfer to the freezer to freeze solid. Then place 1 scoop of Vanilla Bean Frozen Yogurt on a cookie and top with a second cookie. Gently press together to form a cookie ice cream sandwich.

8. Individually wrap the cookie sandwiches and store in a freezer-safe container in the freezer until ready to enjoy.

Tips & Tidbits

....

Feel free to use any cookie recipe in this book
(or anywhere else, for that matter) to make these
ice cream sandwiches. It's especially fun to create
mismatched cookies, such as pairing an Original
Chocolate Chip Cookie with a Double Chocolate
Chip Cookie. Or an Almost Oatmeal Cookie with a
Snickerdoodle . . . the ideas are endless!

Original Chocolate Chip Cookies

(DFO)

Makes 1½ Dozen Cookies

It's the simple pleasures in life that can bring the most joy. Like baking cookies with your kids that taste just like the ones you grew up baking with your mom and grandma. That's why this Original Chocolate Chip Cookies recipe is by far one of my personal favorites. It tastes so close to the recipe on those famous packaged chocolate chips that you'll reminisce about the past with each wonderful bite.

1¾ cups blanched almond flour

1 teaspoon coconut flour

¼ teaspoon baking soda

¼ scant teaspoon sea salt

3 tablespoons unsalted butter, softened, (or palm shortening)

2 tablespoons coconut oil

⅓ cup coconut crystals

1 teaspoon pure vanilla extract

1 large egg

⅓ cup dairy-free mini chocolate chips

1. Preheat oven to 350°F. Line a baking sheet with parchment paper. In a small bowl, combine the almond flour, coconut flour, baking soda, and salt.

2. In a large mixing bowl, add the butter (or palm shortening), coconut oil, coconut crystals, and vanilla. Using a stand mixer or electric hand mixer, blend together until smooth and creamy. Then mix in the egg until well incorporated.

3. Add the dry ingredients to the wet and mix well to combine. Using a rubber spatula, fold in the chocolate chips.

4. Drop the dough by rounded spoonfuls at least 2" apart onto the parchment-lined baking sheet. Use your fingers to slightly flatten the cookies.

5. Bake for 8–10 minutes, until lightly browned along edges. Allow the cookies to cool on the cookie sheet for 5 minutes, then transfer to a wire rack to finish cooling.

Tips & Tidbits

Nearly all cookie dough is perfect for freezing. So why not make a double or triple batch and freeze the extra dough for future baking? Simply drop dough by rounded tablespoonfuls about 1" apart on a parchment-lined baking sheet and place in freezer. Once the dough balls are frozen solid, place them into a freezer-safe container and return to the freezer. When ready to bake, all you have to do is place frozen cookie dough balls on a parchment-lined baking sheet, and allow them to thaw. Then bake as directed in the recipe.

Double Chocolate Chip Cookies

(DFO)

Makes 1½ Dozen Cookies

This recipe turns the chocolatey flavor of my Original Chocolate Chip Cookies (see recipe in this chapter) up a notch or two thanks to the rich, decadent taste of cocoa powder. The addition of walnuts provides a crunchy balance of flavor and texture that works especially well with this recipe. It's definitely a special treat chocolate lovers will enjoy.

1½ cups blanched almond flour

¼ teaspoon baking soda

¼ scant teaspoon sea salt

¼ cup unsalted butter, softened, (or palm shortening)

2 tablespoons coconut oil

½ cup, plus 1 tablespoon coconut crystals

¼ cup unsweetened cocoa powder

1 teaspoon pure vanilla extract

1 large egg white

½ cup dairy-free mini chocolate chips

⅓ cup walnut pieces

1. Preheat oven to 350°F. Line a baking sheet with parchment paper. In a small bowl, combine the almond flour, baking soda, and salt.

2. In a large mixing bowl, add the butter (or palm shortening), coconut oil, coconut crystals, unsweetened cocoa powder, and vanilla. Using a stand mixer or electric hand mixer, blend together until smooth and creamy. Then mix in the egg white until well incorporated.

3. Add the dry ingredients to the wet and mix well to combine. Using a rubber spatula, fold in the chocolate chips and walnut pieces.

4. Drop the dough by rounded spoonfuls at least 2" apart onto the parchment-lined baking sheet. Use your fingers to slightly flatten the cookies.

5. Bake for 8–10 minutes, until lightly browned along edges. Allow the cookies to cool on the cookie sheet for 5 minutes, then transfer to a wire rack to finish cooling.

Almond Flour Thumbprints

Makes 2½ Dozen Cookies

Sweet and pretty, these Almond Flour Thumbprint cookies most often appear during the holiday season. They're best served within a few hours of baking, since honey-sweetened almond flour cookies tend to soften as they sit at room temperature. Of course, this is rarely an issue—they tend to be quickly gobbled up since they're so delicious!

2½ cups blanched almond flour
¼ teaspoon baking soda
¼ scant teaspoon salt
⅓ cup coconut oil
¼ cup honey
1 teaspoon pure vanilla extract
Assorted all-fruit jams for filling cookies

1. In a small bowl, combine the almond flour, baking soda, and salt.

2. In a large mixing bowl, add the coconut oil, honey, and vanilla. Using a stand mixer or electric hand mixer, blend together until smooth and creamy.

3. Add the dry ingredients to the wet and mix well to combine. Chill the dough for 30 minutes in the fridge.

4. Meanwhile, preheat oven to 350°F. Line a baking sheet with parchment paper and gather an assortment of whatever all-fruit jams you have on hand.

5. Once the dough is chilled, scoop out tablespoon-sized portions and roll into balls using your hands. Place the cookie balls onto the parchment-lined baking sheet and slightly flatten using the palm of your hand. Using your thumb (or a ¼-size teaspoon), gently press each cookie to form a small well in the center to hold the jam, then add a small dot of jam (about ⅛ of a teaspoon) in the center of each cookie.

6. Bake for 8–10 minutes, until cookies begin to slightly brown along edges. Allow to cool on baking sheet for 5 minutes. Then transfer to a wire rack to finish cooling.

Holiday Cookie Cut-Outs

(DFO) (EF) (SCD)

Makes 1½ Dozen Cookies

When it comes to the holidays, cookies aren't optional—they're a must! It's not about indulging in sweets (well, maybe a little), as much as it is about the joy of building fond memories and family traditions. The fact is, you can absolutely enjoy the fun holiday tradition of decorating cookies without compromising good health if you choose a real-food cookie recipe like this one and top it with naturally sweet decorating options.

2½ cups blanched almond flour

2 teaspoons coconut flour

¼ teaspoon baking soda

¼ scant teaspoon salt

¼ cup unsalted butter, softened, (or palm shortening)

2 tablespoons coconut oil

¼ cup honey

2 teaspoons vanilla extract

1 batch of The Best Cookie Icing (see recipe in Chapter 10)

Optional: Dried fruits, nuts, and unsweetened coconut for decorating

1. In a small bowl, combine the almond flour, coconut flour, baking soda, and salt.

2. In a large mixing bowl, add the butter (or palm shortening), coconut oil, honey, and vanilla. Using a stand mixer or electric hand mixer, blend together until smooth and creamy.

3. Slowly add the dry ingredients, and continue to mix until thoroughly combined.Chill dough in refrigerator at least 1 hour (or up to 24 hours).

4. Preheat oven to 325°F. Line a baking sheet with parchment paper and set aside.

5. Divide dough in half. Place half on a large sheet of parchment paper. Keep other half of dough in the bowl and return to the fridge to stay cold.

6. Cover the dough with a second sheet of parchment. Roll out the dough to ¼" thick. Remove parchment and use your favorite cookie cutters to cut shapes into the dough. Do not remove the cookie cut-outs, but instead slide the parchment onto a baking sheet and place in the freezer for a few minutes to harden.

7. Once slightly hardened, remove from freezer and gently separate your almost-frozen cookie cut-outs from the dough and place them onto

a second parchment-lined baking sheet to bake. (This simple process makes it much easier to transfer the sticky cookies without them losing their shape.)

8. Form the scrap-dough into a ball and place back in fridge to re-chill. Remove other half of chilled dough and repeat process of rolling and cutting out dough until all dough is used.

9. Bake for 6–8 minutes, until cookies begin to slightly brown along edges. Allow cookies to cool on baking sheet for 5 minutes. Then transfer to a wire rack to finish cooling.

10. To decorate the cookie cut-outs, use The Best Cookie Icing to create beautiful designs. Or use a variety of dried fruits—cutting them into small bits and strips—as well as nuts and unsweetened shredded coconut.

Tips & Tidbits

These cookies are best served within an hour or so of baking, since honey-sweetened almond flour cookies tend to soften fairly quickly as they sit at room temperature. However, they do freeze well and there's no need to defrost—you can enjoy them frozen right from the freezer.

Sugar Cookie Cut-Outs

Makes 1 Dozen Cookies

For those who are able to indulge in a little coconut sugar, these delectable cookies are a crisper option to the Holiday Cookie Cut-Outs (see recipe in this chapter). Have fun decorating these with an assortment of dried fruits and nuts, as well as a few decorative swirls of my dairy-free cookie icing.

2¼ cups blanched almond flour

¼ teaspoon baking soda

¼ scant teaspoon sea salt

¼ cup unsalted butter, softened (or palm shortening)

¼ cup coconut oil, softened

⅓ cup, plus 1 tablespoon coconut crystals

½ teaspoon pure almond extract

1 batch of The Best Cookie Icing (see recipe in Chapter 10)

Optional: Dried fruits, nuts, and unsweetened coconut for decorating

1. In a small bowl, combine the almond flour, baking soda, and salt.

2. In a large mixing bowl, add the butter (or palm shortening), coconut oil, coconut crystals, and almond extract. Using a stand mixer or electric hand mixer, blend together until smooth and creamy.

3. Slowly add the dry ingredients, and continue to mix until thoroughly combined. Chill dough in refrigerator at least 1 hour, or up to 24 hours.

4. Preheat oven to 325°F. Line a baking sheet with parchment paper and set aside.

5. Divide dough in half. Place half on a large sheet of parchment paper. Keep other half of dough in the bowl and return to the fridge to stay cold.

6. Cover the dough with a second sheet of parchment. Then roll out the dough to ¼" thick. Use your favorite cookie cutters to cut shapes into the dough. Do not remove the cookie cut-outs, but instead slide the parchment onto a baking sheet and place in the freezer for a few minutes to harden.

7. Once slightly hardened, remove from freezer and gently separate your almost-frozen cookie cut-outs from the dough and place them onto a second parchment-lined baking sheet. (This simple process makes it much easier to transfer the sticky cookies without them losing their shape.)

8. Form the scrap-dough into a ball and place back in fridge to re-chill. Remove other half of chilled dough and repeat process of rolling and cutting out dough until all dough is used.

9. Bake for 6–8 minutes, until cookies begin to slightly brown along edges. Allow cookies to cool on baking sheet for 5 minutes. Then transfer to a wire rack to finish cooling.

10. To decorate the cookie cut-outs, use The Best Cookie Icing to create beautiful designs. Or use a variety of dried fruits—cutting them into small bits and strips—as well as crispy nuts and unsweetened shredded coconut.

Gingerbread Boys and Girls

(DFO) (EF)

Makes 1½ Dozen Cookies

These delicious cookies were developed specifically so you and your family can enjoy making gingerbread men (or "Gingerbread Boys and Girls," as we call them) without the use of processed ingredients. And not only are the cookies themselves wholesome, but you can easily bypass traditional sugary icings and candies and instead decorate them using dried fruits and nuts, or with a little of my honey-sweetened, dairy-free cookie icing.

2½ cups blanched almond flour

1 tablespoon ground ginger

½ teaspoon ground cinnamon

⅛ teaspoon ground nutmeg

¼ teaspoon baking soda

¼ teaspoon sea salt

3 tablespoons unsalted butter, melted, (or palm shortening)

2 tablespoons coconut oil, melted

2 tablespoons organic unsulfured molasses

⅓ cup pure maple syrup (or ¼ cup honey)

½ teaspoon pure vanilla extract

1 batch of The Best Cookie Icing (see recipe in Chapter 10)

Optional: Dried fruits, nuts, and unsweetened coconut for decorating

1. In a small bowl, combine the almond flour, spices, baking soda, and salt.

2. In a large mixing bowl, add the butter (or palm shortening), coconut oil, molasses, maple syrup (or honey), and vanilla. Using a stand mixer or electric hand mixer, blend together until smooth and creamy.

3. Slowly add the dry ingredients, and continue to mix until thoroughly combined. Chill dough in refrigerator at least 1 hour, or up to 24 hours.

4. Preheat oven to 350°F. Line a baking sheet with parchment paper and set aside.

5. Divide dough in half. Place half on a large sheet of parchment paper. Keep other half of dough in the bowl and return to the fridge to stay cold.

6. Cover the dough with a second sheet of parchment. Then roll out the dough to ¼" thick. Use your favorite cookie cutters to cut shapes into the dough. Do not remove the cookie cut-outs, but instead slide the parchment onto a baking sheet and place in the freezer for a few minutes to harden.

7. Once slightly hardened, remove from freezer and gently separate your almost-frozen cookie cut-outs from the dough and place them onto a second parchment-lined baking sheet. (This simple process makes it much easier to transfer the sticky cookies without them losing their shape.)

8. Form the scrap-dough into a ball and place back in fridge to re-chill. Remove other half of chilled dough and repeat process of rolling and cutting out dough until all dough is used.

9. Bake for 7–10 minutes, until cookies begin to slightly brown along edges. Allow cookies to cool on baking sheet for 5 minutes. Then transfer to a wire rack to finish cooling.

10. To decorate the cookie cut-outs, use The Best Cookie Icing to create beautiful designs. Or use a variety of dried fruits—cutting them into small bits and strips—as well as crispy nuts and unsweetened shredded coconut.

Chapter

9

BROWNIES AND BARS

Coconut Flour Brownies

Makes 9 Bars

This dark chocolate brownie is so rich, it's best served with a simple dollop of Whipped Coconut Cream. However, if you're a chocoholic, you'll definitely want to top this treat with my ultra-decadent Chocolate Ganache icing.

½ cup coconut flour

¼ teaspoon baking soda

¼ teaspoon sea salt

⅓ cup coconut oil

¼ cup unsalted butter (or palm shortening)

½ cup dairy-free mini chocolate chips

1 tablespoon cocoa powder

½ cup honey

½ cup coconut milk

2 large eggs

1 teaspoon pure vanilla extract

Optional: **Whipped Coconut Cream or Chocolate Ganache for topping brownies (see recipes in Chapter 10)**

1. Preheat oven to 350°F. Lightly oil an 8" × 8" baking dish; set aside.

2. In a small bowl, mix together the coconut flour, baking soda, and salt; set aside.

3. Place the coconut oil and butter (or palm shortening) in a small saucepan and melt over low heat. Add the chocolate chips, cocoa powder, and honey. Stir the mixture until the chocolate chips begin to soften. Then remove from heat and continue stirring until the chocolate chips are completely melted and the mixture is well combined. Set aside to cool.

4. In a large bowl, add the coconut milk, eggs, and vanilla. Whisk together until well combined. Then slowly whisk in the cooled chocolate mixture, using a rubber spatula to get all of the chocolate mixture out of the saucepan.

5. Sift the dry ingredients into the wet while whisking vigorously. Continue whisking until no lumps remain. Allow the batter to rest about 5 minutes so the coconut flour can absorb some of the liquid. Then pour the brownie batter into the prepared baking dish.

6. Bake for approximately 25 minutes, just until a toothpick inserted into center comes out clean. Remove from oven and allow to cool completely in the baking dish, then cut into bars. Top with Whipped Coconut Cream, if desired. Or, for an ultra-chocolatey treat, top with my decadent Chocolate Ganache.

Decadent Fudgy Brownies

(DFO)

Makes 9 Bars

Sometimes you just gotta have a brownie! And, whether you're grain-free or not, these decadent fudgy brownies are everything a brownie should be—chewy, gooey, and rich with chocolatey goodness. For an extra special treat, top these with a scoop of homemade Vanilla Bean Frozen Yogurt.

¾ cup blanched almond flour

1 teaspoon coconut flour

¼ teaspoon baking soda

¼ teaspoon sea salt

½ cup unsalted butter (or palm shortening)

½ cup dairy-free mini chocolate chips

3 tablespoons unsweetened cocoa powder

3 large eggs, room temperature

½ cup honey

2 teaspoons pure vanilla extract

Optional: Vanilla Bean Frozen Yogurt for topping brownies (see recipe in Chapter 10)

1. Preheat oven to 340°F. Very lightly oil an 8" × 8" baking dish.

2. In a small bowl, mix together the almond flour, coconut flour, baking soda, and salt; set aside.

3. Cut the butter into chunks. Then place the butter chunks (or palm shortening) into a small saucepan and melt over medium heat. Add the chocolate chips and the cocoa powder. Stir until the chocolate chips begin to soften. Then remove from heat and continue stirring until the chocolate chips are completely melted and the mixture is well combined. Set aside to cool.

4. In a large bowl, add the eggs, honey, and vanilla. Whisk together until well combined. Then slowly whisk in the cooled chocolate mixture, using a rubber spatula to get all of the chocolate mixture out of the saucepan.

5. Slowly add the dry ingredients to the wet while whisking vigorously. Continue whisking until no lumps remain.

6. Pour the batter into the prepared baking dish and use a spreader to even out the top, if needed.

7. Bake for approximately 25–28 minutes until a toothpick inserted into center comes out clean. Remove from oven and allow to cool completely in the baking dish, then cut into bars and serve.

8. For an extra special treat, top with a scoop of Vanilla Bean Frozen Yogurt, if desired.

Recipe Variation

....

This recipe makes lovely brownie bites as well. Simply oil a 24-cup mini-muffin tin with palm shortening. Follow all directions in the recipe, except preheat the oven to 325°F and bake for approximately 15 minutes. Allow brownie bites to cool in pan about 5 minutes. Then run a knife around each brownie bite and slide out while they're still slightly warm. Yum!

The Ultimate Cookie Bars

(DFO)

Makes 9 Bars

This deliciously whimsical bar is a match made in heaven! It combines two classic favorites—chocolate chip cookies and brownies—into a rich and glorious treat that definitely brings the "wow" factor to any party or special occasion.

CHOCOLATE CHIP COOKIE LAYER

1½ cups blanched almond flour

½ teaspoon baking soda

¼ teaspoon sea salt

¼ cup unsalted butter (or coconut oil), softened

¼ cup honey

1 large egg

1 teaspoon pure vanilla extract

2 tablespoons dairy-free mini chocolate chips

FUDGY BROWNIE LAYER

½ cup blanched almond flour

¼ teaspoon baking soda

¼ teaspoon sea salt

¼ cup unsalted butter (or coconut oil)

⅓ cup pure honey

⅓ cup dairy-free mini chocolate chips

2 tablespoons unsweetened cocoa powder

2 large eggs

1 teaspoon pure vanilla extract

Optional: Chocolate chips, walnuts, and unsweetened shredded coconut for topping the bars

1. Preheat oven to 340°F. Lightly oil an 8" × 8" baking dish; set aside.

2. **For the Chocolate Chip Cookie Layer:** In a small bowl, mix together the almond flour, baking soda, and salt. Set aside.

3. In a large mixing bowl, add the butter (or coconut oil) and honey. Using a stand mixer or electric hand mixer, blend together until creamy. Add the egg and vanilla and continue to mix until well blended.

4. Add the dry ingredients and continue to mix until incorporated. Using a rubber spatula, fold in the chocolate chips. Then use an angled cake spatula (spreader) to smooth the cookie dough evenly across the bottom of the prepared 8" × 8" baking dish; set aside.

5. **For the Fudgy Brownie Layer:** In a small bowl, mix together the almond flour, baking soda, and salt; set aside.

6. Place the butter (or coconut oil) in a small saucepan and melt over low heat. Add the honey, chocolate chips, and cocoa powder. Stir the mixture until the chocolate chips begin to soften. Then remove from heat and continue stirring until the chocolate chips are completely melted and the mixture is well combined. Set aside to cool.

7. In a large bowl, add the eggs and vanilla. Whisk together until well combined. Then slowly whisk in the cooled chocolate mixture, using a rubber spatula to get all of the chocolate mixture out of the saucepan.

8. Add the dry ingredients to the wet while whisking vigorously. Continue whisking until no lumps remain.

9. Pour the brownie batter over the chocolate chip cookie dough. For an extra special touch, sprinkle top of batter with a handful of chocolate chips, walnut pieces, and unsweetened shredded coconut.

10. Bake for approximately 28–30 minutes until a toothpick inserted into center comes out with a moist crumb. (It's okay if the center is a bit fudgy. Do not overbake.) Remove from oven and allow the bars to cool completely in the baking dish before cutting and serving. Then cut into 9 bars and enjoy!

Peach Cobbler Breakfast Bars

Makes 9 Bars

In the summer, when peaches are in season, these scrumptious bars are a favorite weekend breakfast treat. In this dish, delicate juicy peach slices barely peek out of a buttery cakelike bar filled with crunchy walnuts and just a touch of cinnamon.

1¼ cups blanched almond flour

2 tablespoons coconut flour

½ teaspoon baking soda

¼ teaspoon sea salt

3 tablespoons unsalted butter, softened (or palm shortening)

3 tablespoons honey

2 large eggs

1 teaspoon pure vanilla extract

⅛ teaspoon ground cinnamon

1 fresh ripe peach, peeled and sliced thinly

¼ cup walnut pieces

1. Preheat oven to 300°F. Lightly oil an 8" × 8" baking dish; set aside.

2. In a small bowl, combine the almond flour, coconut flour, baking soda, and salt. Set aside.

3. In a large mixing bowl, add the butter (or palm shortening) and honey. Using a stand mixer or electric hand mixer, blend together until well combined. Add the eggs and vanilla and continue to mix until well incorporated.

4. Add the dry ingredients to the butter mixture and mix well to combine.

5. Spoon batter into the prepared baking dish, making sure to leave about 1 cup of batter in the bowl.

6. Mix the cinnamon into the cup of reserved batter. Then fold in the peaches and walnuts.

7. Use a spreader to even out the top of the batter in the baking dish first, then spoon the peach mixture on top and even out that layer as well.

8. Bake for 30–35 minutes until golden brown and a toothpick inserted into center comes out clean. Allow to cool before cutting into bars.

Tips & Tidbits

Out of peaches? No worries! These bars taste wonderful made with soft ripe pear slices as well.

Pumpkin Praline Bars

Makes 9 Bars

At the first hint of fall, my favorite recipes to bake are those containing pumpkin purée and mulling spices! You'll find both in these ultra-moist and flavorful bars. In fact, there's nothing that says fall like the mouthwatering aroma and taste of these healthy, pumpkin-rich treats!

PUMPKIN BARS

1 cup blanched almond flour

1 teaspoon coconut flour

½ teaspoon baking soda

¼ teaspoon sea salt

½ cup pumpkin purée

⅓ cup honey

2 large eggs

1½ teaspoons Pumpkin Pie Spice (see recipe in Chapter 10)

¼ teaspoon pure vanilla extract

PRALINE TOPPING

1 tablespoon butter (or coconut oil), melted

2 teaspoons honey

⅛ teaspoon ground cinnamon

⅓ cup pecan pieces

1. Preheat oven to 350°F. Lightly oil an 8" × 8" baking dish; set aside.

2. **For the Pumpkin Bars:** In a small bowl, combine the almond flour, coconut flour, baking soda, and salt. Set aside.

3. In a large mixing bowl, add the pumpkin, honey, eggs, Pumpkin Pie Spice, and vanilla. Using a stand mixer or electric hand mixer, blend together until well combined.

4. Add the dry ingredients to the wet and continue to mix until well combined. Then spoon the batter into the prepared baking dish and use an offset spatula to even out the top.

5. **For the Praline Topping:** In a small bowl, add the butter (or coconut oil), honey, and cinnamon. Whisk well to combine. Add the pecan pieces and toss well to coat.

6. Sprinkle the praline topping evenly across the top of the pumpkin bar batter, making sure to gently press it into the batter a bit.

7. Bake for 22–25 minutes, until a toothpick inserted into center comes out clean. Allow to cool before cutting into bars.

Raspberry Crumble Bars

Makes 16 Bars

This summertime favorite highlights the sweet and tangy flavor of raspberries. And although there are several steps, these bars come together very easily, making them the perfect dessert for summer entertaining. They also freeze well, if you can resist the temptation of eating them all in one sitting!

COOKIE CRUST

1½ cups blanched almond flour
½ teaspoon baking soda
¼ teaspoon sea salt
¼ cup unsalted butter (or coconut oil), melted
1 tablespoon pure honey
1 teaspoon pure vanilla extract
1 tablespoon coconut flour
½ cup raspberry jam (or preserves)

CRUMBLE TOPPING

3 tablespoons butter (or coconut oil), melted
1 teaspoon pure honey
¾ cup blanched almond flour
½ cup unsweetened finely shredded coconut
3–4 tablespoons sliced almonds

1. Preheat the oven to 325°F. Lightly oil bottom and sides of an 8" × 8" baking dish. Then trim parchment paper in a long strip so that it not only lines the bottom but also hangs over 2 sides of the dish. (This will allow you to lift the uncut bar mixture out of the dish once baked and cooled.)

2. **For the Cookie Crust:** In a small bowl, combine the almond flour, baking soda, and salt. Set aside.

3. In a medium mixing bowl, whisk together the melted butter (or coconut oil), honey, and vanilla. Then whisk in the coconut flour.

4. Stir the blanched almond flour mixture into the butter mixture. Mix with a spoon until well combined. (The dough will be crumbly, but should be moist enough that it sticks together when you pinch it.) Spoon the dough into the prepared baking dish and press it evenly along the bottom to form the crust.

5. Bake the crust for 5–6 minutes, just until it rises a bit. Remove from oven, but do not turn oven off. Spoon the jam over the hot crust and spread evenly, making sure to leave about ¼" of bare crust on all sides. This prevents the jam from seeping under the crust.

6. **For the Crumble Topping:** In the same bowl you used for the crust, whisk together the melted butter (or coconut oil) and honey.

7. Using a spoon, stir in the blanched almond flour and shredded coconut until incorporated but still a bit crumbly. Then using your fingers, evenly crumble the coconut topping over the top of the preserves. Next, evenly scatter the sliced almonds across the top. Gently press the almonds into the crumble topping a bit.

8. Bake for 18–20 minutes, until the crumble topping is light golden brown. Cool completely. Then transfer to the refrigerator to chill, about 2–3 hours.

9. Once chilled, remove from fridge and run a knife along the 2 sides without parchment. Using the parchment, gently lift the bar-flat out of the dish and place on a cutting board. Cut into 16 bars and enjoy!

Tips & Tidbits

Wrap any leftover bars and store in the
fridge for up to a week, or in the freezer
for up to 1 month. Also note that you can
use any jam or preserves you prefer to
create these delicious layer bars. Some
of our other favorites are apricot, mixed
berry, and strawberry.

Luscious Lemon Squares

Makes 9 Bars

My personal favorite treat is anything lemon. I just adore its tangy flavor. It takes a bit more time to make these Luscious Lemon Squares than it would to make a typical lemon bar because they're made with freshly prepared lemon curd. However, I assure you that it's worth the extra few minutes. The burst of lemony goodness paired with a light, cookie-like crust make this dessert a scrumptious summertime treat!

CRUST

1¾ cups blanched almond flour

3 tablespoons unsalted butter, cut into pieces, (or palm shortening)

1 teaspoon coconut flour

¼ teaspoon baking soda

⅛ teaspoon sea salt

2 tablespoons honey

¼ teaspoon pure vanilla extract

LEMON CURD FILLING

6 large egg yolks, room temperature

½ cup honey

1 teaspoon lemon zest

½ cup fresh-squeezed lemon juice

¼ teaspoon pure vanilla extract

6 tablespoons unsalted butter, cut into pieces, (or palm shortening)

Optional: Unsweetened shredded coconut for sprinkling on tops of bars

1. Preheat oven to 315°F. Lightly oil bottom and sides of an 8" × 8" baking dish. Then trim parchment paper in a long strip so that it not only lines the bottom but also hangs over 2 sides of the dish. (This will allow you to lift the uncut bar mixture out of the dish once baked and cooled.)

2. **For the Crust:** Place the almond flour, butter pieces (or palm shortening), coconut flour, baking soda, and salt into the bowl of a food processor and pulse 6–8 times. Then add the honey and vanilla and pulse until it starts to form a dough ball.

3. Use a rubber spatula to remove the dough and place into the prepared baking dish. Press the dough evenly into the bottom of the dish.

4. Bake crust for 8–10 minutes, until puffy but not browned. Remove from oven, but do not turn oven off. Allow crust to cool before filling.

5. **For the Lemon Curd Filling:** In a small saucepan, whisk together the egg yolks, honey, lemon zest, lemon juice, and vanilla until well blended.

6. Heat the mixture over low heat and slowly add the butter (or palm shortening) 1 tablespoon at a time, while continually stirring. Be sure to wait until each one melts before adding the next.

7. After all the butter (or palm shortening) is melted and incorporated, continue to cook, stirring frequently, until it thickens like a thin pudding. Then remove from the heat.

8. Pour the warm lemon curd through a fine mesh strainer into a small bowl. Transfer to the refrigerator to cool.

9. Once cool to touch (not cold), add the lemon curd to the cooled crust, using an offset spatula to smooth it out evenly.

10. Bake at 315°F for approximately 20 minutes, until filling sets and slightly puffs up. Remove from oven and allow to cool about 20 minutes. Then cover and refrigerate for at least 2–3 hours, or overnight.

11. Once cold, remove from fridge. Run a knife along the 2 edges without parchment. Using the parchment paper ends, lift the dessert from the baking dish and place on a cutting board. Cut into 9 bars and enjoy. For a decorative touch, sprinkle the bars with unsweetened shredded coconut, if desired.

Tips & Tidbits

Whenever a recipe calls for lemon zest, lemon juice, or both, I always zest the lemons first and then extract the juice. Then I measure out what I need for the recipe and place the remaining zest and juice in freezer-safe containers for use in future recipes. Taking a quick minute to do this not only helps to eliminate waste, but also saves prep time for future recipes.

Fruit and Nut Snack Bars

Makes 8 Bars

Inspired by my affinity for those conveniently packaged fruit and nut bars, this honey-sweetened, grain-free version is far less expensive to make. Even better, you can customize the recipe to make a wide variety of flavor combinations based on your own personal taste preferences.

⅓ cup honey

2 tablespoons coconut flour

1 tablespoon all-natural almond butter

⅛ teaspoon sea salt

1⅓ cups unsalted chopped whole nuts of your choice (such as almonds, cashews, and pistachios)

½ cup chopped dried fruit of your choice (such as raisins, currants, cranberries, and blueberries)

1 cup unsweetened coconut flakes (not shredded coconut)

1. Preheat oven to 300°F. Lightly oil bottom and sides of an 8" × 8" baking dish. Then trim parchment paper in a long strip so that it not only lines the bottom but also hangs over 2 sides of the dish. (This will allow you to lift the uncut bar mixture out of the dish once baked and cooled.)

2. In a large bowl, add the honey, coconut flour, nut butter, and salt. Use a spoon to stir until well combined. Then add the chopped nuts and dried fruit to the honey mixture; set aside.

3. Place coconut flakes on the cutting board and coarse-chop. Add chopped coconut flakes to honey mixture. Using a spoon, mix ingredients together, making sure they are thoroughly combined.

4. Place the bar mixture into the parchment-lined baking dish. Fold overlapping flaps down and evenly press the top of the bar mixture firmly to pack in the ingredients so they hold together better after baking. Then peel back the parchment flaps from top of bar mixture. (Do not trim, as the flaps make it easier to remove the bar mixture after baking.)

5. Bake for 20 minutes until very lightly browned at edges. Then remove from oven and allow to completely cool on stovetop for approximately 1 hour, or until bottom of baking dish is room temperature. Place in fridge to continue cooling. (Do not freeze, as this makes it impossible to cut the bars without them crumbling.)

6. Once cold, remove dish from refrigerator. Then run a knife along the 2 edges without parchment. Using the parchment paper ends, lift the bar-flat from the baking dish and place on a cutting board. Cut into 8 bars and individually wrap and store in the fridge or freezer. For best results, bars should be kept cold so they do not become too sticky. Simply include an ice pack, if taking them on the go.

Tips & Tidbits

You can use any combination of nuts you like; just be sure to rough-chop the nuts first and then measure out 1⅓ cups. (Soaked and dehydrated nuts are best, especially for those with digestive issues.) Our favorite combination is almonds, cashews, and pistachios paired with dried cranberries and dried wild blueberries as shown in the photo.

Nut-Free Snack Bars

DF **EF** **NF** **SCD**

Makes 8 Bars

Shortly after the recipe for my original Fruit and Nut Snack Bars (see recipe in this chapter) went global, many readers asked if it was possible to make a nut-free version of these popular bars. The answer in short is . . . yes! Made with pepitas (pumpkin seeds) and sunflower seeds, these bars are absolutely scrumptious—whether you're nut-free or not!

⅓ cup pure honey

2 tablespoons coconut flour

1 tablespoon all-natural sunflower seed butter

⅛ teaspoon sea salt

1 cup unsweetened coconut flakes

½ cup chopped dried fruit

1 cup unsalted pepitas (pumpkin seeds)

⅓ cup unsalted sunflower seeds

1. Preheat oven to 300°F. Lightly oil bottom and sides of an 8" × 8" baking dish. Then trim parchment paper in a long strip so that it not only lines the bottom but also hangs over 2 sides of the dish. (This will allow you to lift the uncut bar mixture out of the dish once baked and cooled.)

2. In a large bowl, add the honey, coconut flour, all-natural sunflower seed butter, and salt. Use a spoon to stir until well combined.

3. Place coconut flakes on the cutting board and coarse-chop. Add chopped coconut flakes to honey mixture.

4. Add the chopped dried fruit, pepitas, and sunflower seeds to the honey mixture. Using a spoon, mix ingredients together making sure they are thoroughly combined.

5. Place the bar mixture into the parchment-lined baking dish. Fold overlapping flaps down and evenly press the top of the bar mixture firmly to pack in the ingredients so they hold together better after baking. Then peel back the parchments flaps from top of bar mixture. (Do not trim, as the flaps make it easier to remove the bar mixture after baking.)

6. Bake for 20 minutes, until very lightly browned at edges. Then remove from oven and allow to completely cool on stovetop for approximately 1 hour, or until bottom of baking dish is room temperature. Place in fridge to continue cooling. (Do not freeze, as this makes it impossible to cut the bars without them crumbling.)

7. Once cold, remove dish from refrigerator. Then run a knife along the 2 edges without parchment. Using the parchment paper ends, lift the bar-flat from the baking dish and place on a cutting board. Cut into 8 bars and individually wrap and store in the fridge or freezer. For best results, bars should be kept cold so they do not become too sticky. Simply include an ice pack, if taking them on the go.

Tips & Tidbits

Although coconut is technically not a nut, if you have nut allergies, be sure to talk to your allergist before adding coconut to your diet.

Almond Flour Blondies

(DFO) (SCD)

Makes 9 Bars

One of the easiest and most versatile of recipes, this new spin on the classic blondie is a delicious treat that everyone will enjoy—whether they're grain-free or not. Most people enjoy the hint of coconut in these bars, but you can certainly omit it and still enjoy a tasty treat.

1½ cups blanched almond flour

¼ cup unsweetened shredded coconut

½ teaspoon baking soda

¼ teaspoon sea salt

¼ cup unsalted butter, softened, (or palm shortening)

¼ cup honey

1 large egg

1 teaspoon pure vanilla extract

¼ cup walnut pieces

Optional: 2–3 tablespoons dairy-free mini chocolate chips (omit for SCD)

1. Preheat oven to 325°F. Lightly oil an 8" × 8" baking dish and line bottom with parchment paper.

2. In a small bowl, mix together the almond flour, shredded coconut, baking soda, and salt. Set aside.

3. In a large mixing bowl, add the butter (or palm shortening) and honey. Using a stand mixer or electric hand mixer, blend together until well combined. Then add the egg and vanilla; blend until incorporated.

4. Add the dry ingredients to the wet and mix until well blended. Then use a rubber spatula to fold in the walnut pieces and chocolate chips, if desired.

5. Transfer batter to prepared baking dish and even out the top with the back of the spatula.

6. Bake for 20–25 minutes, until golden brown along edges and a toothpick inserted into center comes out clean. Remove from oven and allow to cool completely. Then cut into 9 bars and serve.

Recipe Variation

By adding an assortment of chopped dried fruits to this recipe, you can create a beautiful and extra-chewy holiday-themed Fruit Cake Blondie. But don't let the name scare you—this is one festive treat that's so delicious, no one will want to re-gift it.

Chapter

10

SWEET ADDITIONS

Classic Vanilla Frosting (DF) (NF) (EF) (SCD)

Creamy Lemon Frosting (DFO) (NF) (SCD)

Lemon Curd (DFO) (NF) (SCD)

Chocolate Cream Frosting (DF) (NF) (EF)

Whipped Coconut Cream
(DF) (NF) (EF) (SCD)

Sweet Vanilla Glaze (DF) (NF) (EF) (SCD)

Chocolate Ganache (DFO) (NF) (EF)

Vanilla Pastry Cream (DF) (NF) (SCD)

Simple Honey-Butter Syrup (NF) (EF) (SCD)

Pumpkin Pie Spice (DF) (NF) (EF) (SCD)

The Best Cookie Icing (DF) (NF) (EF) (SCD)

Vanilla Bean Frozen Yogurt (DFO) (NF) (EF) (SCD)

Whole Milk Yogurt (NF) (EF) (SCD)

Coconut Milk Yogurt (DF) (NF) (EF) (SCD)

Classic Vanilla Frosting

(DF) (NF) (EF) (SCD)

Makes 2 Cups

The fluffy billowy consistency of this dairy-free frosting belies the fact that it can hold its own, even on a warm day. Its creamy, velvety-smooth texture and sweet vanilla flavor make it worthy of topping your most treasured confections.

1 cup palm shortening
⅓ cup coconut butter
½ cup honey
2 teaspoons pure vanilla extract

1. In a large mixing bowl, add the palm shortening and coconut butter. Using a stand mixer fitted with the whisk attachment, or an electric hand mixer, mix at medium-high speed approximately 2 minutes, until fluffy and creamy.

2. Add the honey and vanilla. Whisk on high until frosting is light and fluffy (about 1–2 minutes), scraping down the sides of the bowl as needed.

3. Use immediately, or refrigerate overnight. Just be sure to allow cold frosting to soften a bit at room temperature and then re-whip it for a minute or so to ensure that it's fluffy and easy to spread.

4. This recipe is perfect for frosting 8–10 cupcakes or a small sheet cake. If frosting a layer cake, be sure to double the recipe.

Tips & Tidbits

If you're unfamiliar with palm shortening or coconut butter, be sure to read about them in the "Grain-Free Pantry Essentials" section in Chapter 1. These are the two crucial ingredients that make this icing spectacular!

Creamy Lemon Frosting

Makes 2 Cups

The burst of sweet lemony flavor in this delightful frosting comes from honey-sweetened homemade Lemon Curd. It's one of my favorites for topping summertime cupcakes and cakes, such as my Lemonade Sunshine Cake (see recipe in Chapter 7).

1 cup palm shortening
⅓ cup coconut butter
¾ cup cold Lemon Curd (see recipe in this chapter)
2 tablespoons honey

1. In a large mixing bowl, add the palm shortening and coconut butter. Using a stand mixer fitted with the whisk attachment, or an electric hand mixer, mix at medium-high speed approximately 2 minutes, until fluffy and creamy.

2. Add the Lemon Curd and honey. Continue to mix until frosting is light and fluffy (about 1–2 minutes), scraping down the sides of the bowl as needed.

3. Use immediately, or refrigerate overnight. Just be sure to allow cold frosting to soften a bit at room temperature and then re-whip it for a minute or so to ensure that it's fluffy and easy to spread.

4. This recipe is perfect for frosting 8–10 cupcakes or a small sheet cake. If frosting a layer cake, be sure to double the recipe.

Lemon Curd

Makes 2 Cups

Homemade Lemon Curd makes the perfect base for creating a variety of tangy lemony confections, from cakes and bars to tarts and frostings. Of course, just a dollop of Lemon Curd all on its own is a special way to brighten any biscuit or scone.

8 egg yolks

¾ cup honey

½ cup fresh-squeezed lemon juice

3 teaspoons lemon zest

6 tablespoons butter (or palm shortening)

¼ teaspoon pure vanilla extract

1. Place egg yolks, honey, lemon juice, and zest into a small saucepan. Whisk well to combine.

2. Heat over medium heat, stirring constantly, until mixture is hot. Then add the butter (or palm shortening) 1 tablespoon at a time, while continually stirring. Be sure to wait until each one melts before adding the next.

3. Once all of the butter (or palm shortening) is incorporated, continue cooking the mixture while whisking constantly, until Lemon Curd thickens (about 5–8 minutes). You will know it's ready when you feel resistance as you stir and the mixture becomes very smooth and creamy.

4. Remove from heat and stir in the vanilla. Allow the curd to cool for a couple of minutes, then pour the warm Lemon Curd through a fine mesh strainer into a pint-sized mason jar. Cover and refrigerate.

Tips & Tidbits

If you have extra lemon juice or zest, don't discard it. Instead, freeze it for use in future recipes.

Chocolate Cream Frosting

Makes 2 Cups

This rich, dairy-free Chocolate Cream Frosting adds a decadent touch to layer cakes and cupcakes, as well as brownies. Just be sure to plan ahead, since this frosting must be refrigerated before you whip it into a smooth and creamy consistency that is perfect for topping your favorite treats.

1 cup palm shortening
1 cup dairy-free mini chocolate chips
1 tablespoon coconut butter
2 tablespoons honey

1. Place all ingredients into a small saucepan over low heat. Stir constantly until melted and combined. Remove from heat and transfer to a large mixing bowl to cool.

2. Refrigerate the mixture in the mixing bowl for about 1 hour, until it's thoroughly chilled and is the consistency of thick fudge.

3. Remove mixing bowl with chocolate mixture from fridge. Using a stand mixer fitted with the whisk attachment, or an electric hand mixer, mix at medium high speed approximately 2–3 minutes, until fluffy and creamy, scraping down the sides of the bowl as needed.

4. Use immediately, or refrigerate overnight. Just be sure to allow cold frosting to soften a bit at room temperature and then re-whip it for a minute or so to ensure that it's fluffy and easy to spread.

5. This recipe is perfect for frosting 8–10 cupcakes or a small sheet cake. If frosting a layer cake, be sure to double the recipe.

Tips & Tidbits

Often separation occurs with coconut butter, as the oils in the butter tend to rise to the surface. So, when opening a new jar, be sure to thoroughly stir the oil back into the coconut butter before using it in a recipe.

Whipped Coconut Cream

Makes 2 Cups

Whipped coconut cream is the perfect replacement for dairy-based whipped toppings, since it's just as smooth and light. Plus, it takes just minutes to whip up and adds a wonderful touch of creamy sweetness to your favorite desserts and beverages.

2 (13.5-ounce) cans pure coconut milk, refrigerated overnight (or 1 (14-ounce) can of pure coconut cream, chilled)

1–2 teaspoons honey

1. Place a large mixing bowl and the beaters (or whisk attachment) into the freezer for 2–3 minutes to thoroughly chill.

2. Remove the cold coconut cream from the 2 cans of cold coconut milk and place into the chilled mixing bowl. An easy way to do this is to open the cans from the bottom and carefully pour off the coconut water into a small mason jar for another use. This makes it easier to scoop out just the coconut cream. Or you can use pure coconut cream instead, which does not require removing the coconut water.

3. Using a stand mixer fitted with the whisk attachment, or an electric mixer, mix at high speed approximately 2–3 minutes, until fluffy and creamy.

4. Add the honey and continue to mix until the coconut cream is light and fluffy (about 1–2 minutes), scraping down the sides of the bowl as needed.

5. Use immediately, or refrigerate for up to 2 days. Just be sure to whip cold coconut cream for a minute or so before using to ensure that it's light and fluffy.

Tips & Tidbits

It's a good idea to keep a couple of cans of coconut milk (or pure coconut cream) in your refrigerator so you always have it on hand for recipes such as this one.

Sweet Vanilla Glaze

(DF) (NF) (EF) (SCD)

Makes ½ Cup

This easy-to-make dairy-free glaze is a delightful addition to cakes, quick breads, and muffins. It not only adds a hint of sweet vanilla goodness but also provides lots of eye appeal. With just a little swirl of this exquisite glaze, you can magically transform any baked good into a party-perfect treat!

1 tablespoon, plus 1 teaspoon raw honey

2 teaspoons coconut oil

½ teaspoon pure vanilla extract

½ cup coconut cream (see Tips & Tidbits for more information)

1. Place the honey, coconut oil, and vanilla in a mixing bowl. Using a stand mixer fitted with the whisk attachment, or an electric mixer, mix at medium speed until well combined and creamy. Then mix in the cold coconut cream just until the mixture is well combined.

2. You can use the glaze by either spooning the mixture over your baked treat or transferring the glaze to a pastry bag or plastic food storage bag (snip one of the corners to pipe) and swirl over your favorite treats. If you opt to pipe the glaze, place it in the fridge for an hour or so to firm up a bit. Or store it in the fridge up to 1–2 days, then allow it to soften a bit at room temperature before decorating.

Tips & Tidbits

Getting coconut cream is easy. Simply place 1 can of coconut milk into the fridge overnight. By chilling the can of coconut milk, the coconut cream will rise to the top of the can. Measure out ½ cup of coconut cream; set aside. Reserve remainder in the fridge for another use.

Chocolate Ganache

Makes 1¼ Cups

Traditional ganache is made using heavy cream and semisweet chocolate. However, this renegade recipe utilizes a little coconut milk in place of the cream, along with a touch of cocoa powder to create a decadent thick chocolatey icing perfect for topping cakes and brownies. If you're dairy-free, use palm shortening in place of the butter for equally delicious results!

¼ cup butter (or palm shortening)
½ cup dairy-free mini chocolate chips
1 tablespoon cocoa powder
1 tablespoon coconut milk
¼ cup honey

1. In a small saucepan over low heat, melt the butter (or palm shortening).

2. Once melted, turn off the heat and add the chocolate chips, slowly whisking until melted.

3. Move pan to a cool area on the stovetop and whisk in the cocoa powder, coconut milk, and honey.

4. Allow mixture to cool to room temperature. Then spoon over your favorite cake or brownies. Use an angled cake spatula to evenly distribute the icing.

5. In order for the icing to fully set, you can leave the dessert at room temperature for several hours before serving. Or you can retrigerate your ganache-topped dessert until icing is set (about 20–30 minutes) or overnight.

Vanilla Pastry Cream

Makes 2½ Cups

A delicately flavored, smooth and velvety pastry cream is a classic staple used to fill all sorts of cakes, tarts, and other pastries. My adoration for pastry cream is why you'll find several delightful desserts in this book that call for this confection, such as my Favorite Fruit Tart (Chapter 6).

1 (13.5-ounce) can of pure coconut milk (1¾ cups)
1 teaspoon coconut butter
1¼ teaspoons unflavored gelatin
3 large egg yolks
3 tablespoons honey
1 teaspoon pure vanilla extract

1. In a small saucepan, add the can of coconut milk and coconut butter. Sprinkle the gelatin on the top of the milk. Allow the gelatin to bloom (soften) about 5–10 minutes.

2. Meanwhile, in a small bowl, whisk together the egg yolks, honey, and vanilla. Set aside.

3. Once gelatin has softened, place saucepan over medium heat. Whisk constantly until the milk and gelatin are well combined and milk is warmed.

4. Very slowly add ½ cup of the warm milk to the yolks, whisking constantly to combine. Slowly pour the yolk mixture into the saucepan and whisk thoroughly.

5. Bring the mixture to a gentle simmer and whisk for 2–3 minutes until slightly thickened. Then pour the custard through a fine mesh strainer into a shallow dish to cool.

6. Once cooled, cover with plastic wrap pressed right against the pastry cream. (This will prevent a thick skin from forming on the surface.)

7. Refrigerate for at least 10–12 hours. Once pastry cream is cold and set, whisk thoroughly to loosen so that it's thick and creamy like custard. Then use it in your favorite recipes as desired.

Recipe Variation

For a lighter version of this recipe, once the pastry cream has completely cooled, simply fold in a little Whipped Coconut Cream to taste (see recipe in this chapter).

Simple Honey-Butter Syrup

Makes 1 Cup

This simple syrup makes a wonderful topping for pancakes and waffles for those who follow the Specific Carbohydrate Diet, or for anyone seeking a sweet, buttery alternative to maple syrup.

¼ cup butter
½ cup honey
¼ cup water
Pinch of cinnamon
¼ teaspoon pure vanilla extract

1. In a small saucepan, melt butter over medium heat. Add honey, water, and cinnamon. Whisk well to combine. Heat until hot and steamy, then remove from heat and whisk in vanilla.

2. Allow to cool, and then transfer to a syrup pitcher and serve warm over your favorite pancakes and waffles. Or store in the fridge and rewarm when ready to use.

Tips & Tidbits

When refrigerated, this syrup will separate. Just rewarm, whisk together, and you're ready to enjoy it again!

Pumpkin Pie Spice

Makes ⅓ Cup

Making your own homemade Pumpkin Pie Spice is easy to do, and allows you to customize the blend according to your taste preferences. It also helps to save time when putting together a recipe, since you measure out all of the various spices just once and then have a ready-made spice blend on hand for creating fall-inspired treats.

3 tablespoons ground cinnamon
2 teaspoons ground ginger
2 teaspoons ground nutmeg
1 teaspoon ground allspice
½ teaspoon ground cloves

1. Combine ingredients in a small bowl until well blended.

2. Transfer to a clean recycled spice jar or small mason jar.

3. Use in your favorite fall-inspired recipes.

The Best Cookie Icing

Makes 1¼ Cups

I was a just a wee bit excited when I finally found a way to make a delicious dairy-free, refined-sugar-free icing that is perfect for decorating cookies. What makes this icing so wonderful is the fact that its creamy-smooth consistency allows you to easily pipe it onto cookies without it being too runny. In fact, it will even firm up at room temperature, just like classic royal icing.

1 (13.5-ounce) can pure coconut milk, refrigerated overnight (or 1 (14-ounce) can of pure coconut cream, chilled)

1 tablespoon water

¼ teaspoon unflavored gelatin

½ cup coconut cream

½ cup coconut butter

1 tablespoon palm shortening

¼ cup honey

Optional: All-natural food coloring (such as India Tree brand)

1. Place 1 can of coconut milk into the fridge overnight. By chilling the can of coconut milk, the coconut cream will rise to the top of the can. Measure out ½ cup of coconut cream; set aside. Reserve remainder in the fridge for another use.

2. In a small prep bowl, add the water and sprinkle the unflavored gelatin across the top. Set aside to allow gelatin time to bloom (soften).

3. In a small saucepan, add the coconut cream, coconut butter, palm shortening, and honey. Warm over low heat just until coconut butter is melted. Whisk well to thoroughly combine the ingredients. Then whisk in the gelatin and remove from the heat.

4. Transfer the icing to a mixing bowl. If you'd like to add color, separate the icing into separate mixing bowls and add desired colors. Refrigerate for at least 2–3 hours or overnight.

5. Remove icing from fridge when ready to use. (If you've allowed it to sit in fridge overnight, you'll need to let it sit at room temperature about 5–10 minutes, as it will be very firm.) Transfer icing to a pastry bag with writing tip insert—or place in a plastic food storage bag and snip one of the corners. Then have fun decorating!

Vanilla Bean Frozen Yogurt

Makes 1 Quart

It's easy to justify enjoying a scoop (or two!) of this sweet and creamy frozen dessert! After all, it's made with wholesome yogurt, which provides a healthy dose of beneficial probiotics in every yummy bite.

1 quart plain Whole Milk Yogurt or Coconut Milk Yogurt (see recipes in this chapter)

1 whole vanilla bean

½ cup honey

1 teaspoon pure vanilla extract

1. Place yogurt in large mixing bowl. Carefully cut the vanilla bean in half lengthwise and scrape the tiny black beans out using the tip of your knife. Place them into the bowl of yogurt, then whisk well to combine.

2. Add the honey and vanilla extract. Whisk well until thoroughly combined.

3. Place in the refrigerator to chill at least 6 hours, preferably 12–24 hours.

4. Prepare ice cream maker, then pour the cold yogurt mixture into the ice cream maker. Follow the instructions provided with your ice cream maker to determine churn time.

5. Serve immediately for a delectable soft serve. Or transfer to an airtight container and freeze for at least 4 hours for a firmer frozen yogurt. Either way, this honey-sweetened cultured frozen treat is delicious!

Whole Milk Yogurt

Makes 1 Quart

Making wholesome homemade yogurt is not only easy, it's also a great way to avoid the unhealthy additives found in many commercial brands. Since yogurt is a common ingredient used in many of my recipes, I've included this foolproof method for making creamy whole milk yogurt, which is perfect for helping create fluffy, light baked goods, as well as for enjoying on its own.

4 cups pasteurized organic whole milk (see Tips & Tidbits for more information)

¼ cup plain organic yogurt (or 1 yogurt starter packet)

Optional: 1 to 1½ teaspoons unflavored gelatin (to thicken yogurt)

1. Heat the milk over medium to medium-high heat until it reaches 165°F, making sure to stir the milk constantly. Do not allow the milk to come to a boil.

2. Once the milk comes to temperature, turn off the burner and place the pan on a cooler area on the stovetop. Allow milk to cool to 110°F. (Or place the pan into a sink partially filled with ice water to cool the milk more quickly.)

3. When milk reaches 110°F, thoroughly whisk in the gelatin, if using. (The addition of unflavored gelatin helps to create a thicker, Greek-style yogurt.) Then add the yogurt starter and continue to whisk until thoroughly combined, about 1 minute.

4. Place the yogurt mixture into a yogurt maker, or use another reliable incubation method of your choice and allow yogurt to culture for at least 8–10 hours, or 24 hours if following the SCD.

5. Once it's done culturing, give the yogurt a good whisking to re-blend, and transfer it to the refrigerator to cool completely.

Tips & Tidbits

Check your milk carton and be sure to use only pasteurized milk for this recipe. Yogurt experts do not recommend using ultra-pasteurized (UHT) milk to make yogurt, since the high temperatures used in the UHT process make it unsuitable for culturing. Also note that if you are using gelatin to thicken yogurt, it's normal to see small gelatinous clumps of yellow liquid. This is just the whey that has separated from the milk solids. Simply whisk to gently blend it back into the yogurt.

Coconut Milk Yogurt

DF **NF** **EF** **SCD**

Makes 1 Quart

For those who are dairy-free, it's nearly impossible to find a commercial coconut milk yogurt free of unwanted additives. The good news is that you can easily make your own delicious and healthy yogurt at home. Just be sure to carefully select yogurt cultures that are dairy-free as well.

2 (13.5-ounce) cans pure coconut milk

1 packet of nondairy yogurt starter (or 1 high-quality probiotic capsule)

Optional: 1 to 1½ teaspoons unflavored gelatin (to thicken yogurt)

1. Heat the coconut milk over medium to medium-high heat until it reaches 115°F, making sure to stir the milk constantly. Do not allow the milk to come to a boil.

2. Once the coconut milk comes to temperature, turn off the burner and move the saucepan to a cooler area on the stovetop.

3. Allow milk to cool to 110°F. (This won't take long, since it's such a small temperature difference.)

4. When milk reaches 110°F, thoroughly whisk in the unflavored gelatin, if using. Then add the nondairy yogurt starter and continue to whisk until thoroughly combined, about 1 minute.

5. Place the yogurt mixture into a yogurt maker, or use another reliable incubation method of your choice, and allow yogurt to culture for 10–18 hours. The longer you culture, the more tangy the taste.

6. Once it's done culturing, give the yogurt a good whisking to re-blend, since separation commonly occurs. Cover and transfer to the refrigerator to cool completely.

RESOURCES

I order many of my grain-free pantry essentials via a local AzureStandard.com co-op, as well as through online sources such as Amazon.com. You can find all of my favorite pantry and bakeware products conveniently located in my online store at TheNourishingHome.com. Or to find a local retailer near you, visit the sites below.

GRAIN-FREE PANTRY ESSENTIALS

Blanched Almond Flour
Honeyville (*www.honeyville.com*)

Coconut Butter and Cashew Butter
Artisana Organic Foods
(*www.artisanafoods.com*)

Coconut Flour
Honeyville (*www.honeyville.com*)

Coconut Milk
Natural Value (*www.naturalvalue.com*)

Coconut Oil and Palm Shortening
Tropical Traditions
(*www.tropicaltraditions.com*)

Cocoa Powder and Chocolate Chips
Dagoba Organic Chocolate
(*www.dagobachocolate.com*)

Enjoy Life Foods (*www.enjoylifefoods.com*)

Coconut (shredded and flakes)
Edward & Sons (*www.edwardandsons.com*)

Grass-Fed Gelatin
Great Lakes Gelatin Company
(*www.greatlakesgelatin.com*)

Honey (locally sourced is best)
Honey Pacifica (*www.honeypacifica.com*)

BAKEWARE AND KITCHEN TOOLS

Countertop Appliances and Kitchen Tools
KitchenAid (*www.kitchenaid.com*)

Bakeware and Baking Tools
Williams-Sonoma
(*www.williams-sonoma.com*)

Beautiful Table Linens
Hen House Linens (*www.henhouselinens.com*)

Parchment Paper and Muffin Liners
If You Care (*www.ifyoucare.com*)

U.S./METRIC CONVERSION CHART

VOLUME CONVERSIONS

U.S. Volume Measure	Metric Equivalent
⅛ teaspoon	0.5 milliliter
¼ teaspoon	1 milliliter
½ teaspoon	2 milliliters
1 teaspoon	5 milliliters
½ tablespoon	7 milliliters
1 tablespoon (3 teaspoons)	15 milliliters
2 tablespoons (1 fluid ounce)	30 milliliters
¼ cup (4 tablespoons)	60 milliliters
⅓ cup	90 milliliters
½ cup (4 fluid ounces)	125 milliliters
⅔ cup	160 milliliters
¾ cup (6 fluid ounces)	180 milliliters
1 cup (16 tablespoons)	250 milliliters
1 pint (2 cups)	500 milliliters
1 quart (4 cups)	1 liter (about)

WEIGHT CONVERSIONS

U.S. Weight Measure	Metric Equivalent
½ ounce	15 grams
1 ounce	30 grams
2 ounces	60 grams
3 ounces	85 grams
¼ pound (4 ounces)	115 grams
½ pound (8 ounces)	225 grams
¾ pound (12 ounces)	340 grams
1 pound (16 ounces)	454 grams

OVEN TEMPERATURE CONVERSIONS

Degrees Fahrenheit	Degrees Celsius
200 degrees F	95 degrees C
250 degrees F	120 degrees C
275 degrees F	135 degrees C
300 degrees F	150 degrees C
325 degrees F	160 degrees C
350 degrees F	180 degrees C
375 degrees F	190 degrees C
400 degrees F	205 degrees C
425 degrees F	220 degrees C
450 degrees F	230 degrees C

BAKING PAN SIZES

U.S.	Metric
8 × 1½ inch round baking pan	20 × 4 cm cake tin
9 × 1½ inch round baking pan	23 × 3.5 cm cake tin
11 × 7 × 1½ inch baking pan	28 × 18 × 4 cm baking tin
13 × 9 × 2 inch baking pan	30 × 20 × 5 cm baking tin
2 quart rectangular baking dish	30 × 20 × 3 cm baking tin
15 × 10 × 2 inch baking pan	30 × 25 × 2 cm baking tin (Swiss roll tin)
9 inch pie plate	22 × 4 or 23 × 4 cm pie plate
7 or 8 inch springform pan	18 or 20 cm springform or loose-bottom cake tin
9 × 5 × 3 inch loaf pan	23 × 13 × 7 cm or 2 lb narrow loaf or pâté tin
1½ quart casserole	1.5 liter casserole
2 quart casserole	2 liter casserole

ACKNOWLEDGMENTS

To my loving husband: Thank you for your patience and encouragement. And for all those little things you do each day that practically show how much you care. I love you beyond words!

To my precious boys: Thank you for your constant humor that keeps me from taking life too seriously. And for stepping in like your Dad, with a helping hand and an encouraging word. *"I love you to the moon and back, and back again!"*

To my beautiful Mom: Thank you for your love and support, and for always having such a generous heart. I couldn't have completed this book without the help of my gracious "cleaning fairy."

To my brother Todd: Thank you for your humor, love, and encouragement—you, Kim, and my precious niece and nephews are a special blessing!

To my wonderful extended family: Thank you for all the love and special memories throughout the years. Our strong family ties are a cherished treasure, and are a constant source of inspiration!

To my dear community of readers and faithful fans: Thank you for your overwhelming support in enthusiastically trying my recipes and sharing how they help to transform your health for the better. This book was written for you!

To my amazing friends and neighbors: Your gracious receiving of every single recipe in this book multiple times over is so appreciated. Thank you for being the ultimate taste-testing team!

To my long-time sponsor Honeyville Farms: Thank you for supplying every ounce of grain-free flour used to develop and perfect each of the recipes here, and at The Nourishing Home.

To Hen House Linens: Thank you for supplying the beautiful linens found throughout this book. The beauty you bring to the table is inspiring!

Thank you to all of my blogging friends, especially to Laura, Kristin, Tiffany, Carrie, Ruth, and the Green Ninjas. Your gracious friendship, encouragement, and support mean the world to me!

Special thanks to my agent, Bill Jensen, and to the team at Adams Media. Your guidance and support made this whole process an absolute joy and honor!

Most important, I humbly thank the Lord for allowing me so many opportunities to serve others. I pray that this book will inspire many to seek the true nourishment that only comes from You!

INDEX

WELLES-TURNER MEMORIAL LIBRARY

3 2512 13476 9690

ABOUT THE AUTHOR

KELLY SMITH is the author and creator of the popular grain-free lifestyle blog *The Nourishing Home* (*http://thenourishinghome.com*). Diagnosed with several autoimmune diseases, yet finding no relief from conventional medicine, she soon discovered the healing benefits of whole foods and began her blog to be a source of inspiration for others. Kelly's recipes are grain-free, gluten-free, and free of refined sugars and starches, with minimal to no dairy—making them appropriate for the most common grain-free lifestyles. With a passion for masterfully transforming everyday comfort foods into delicious grain-free creations, Kelly is on a mission to help individuals and families live a more nourished life.